The Sense of Quoting

Biblical Interpretation

Editor-in-Chief

Tat-siong Benny Liew (*College of the Holy Cross*, USA)

Editorial Board

Greg Carey (*Lancaster Theological Seminary*, USA) – Colleen Conway (*Seton Hall University*, USA) – James Crossley (*St. Mary's University*, UK) – Steed Davidson (*McCormick Theological Seminary*, USA) – Rhiannon Graybill (*Rhodes College*, USA) – Jione Havea (*Charles Sturt University, Australia*) – Jacqueline Hidalgo (*Williams College*, USA) – Robert S. Kawashima (*University of Florida*, USA) – Jennifer L. Koosed (*Albright College*, USA) – Francis Landy (*University of Alberta, Canada*) – Davina C. Lopez (*Eckerd College*, USA) – Stephen D. Moore (*Drew University*, USA) – Sarojini Nadar (*University of the Western Cape, South Africa*) – Laura Salah Nasrallah (*Harvard University*, USA) – Jorunn Økland (*University of Oslo, Norway*) – Jeremy Schipper (*Temple University*, USA) – Abraham Smith (*Southern Methodist University*, USA) – Naomi Steinberg (*DePaul University*, USA) – Hannah Strommen (*University of Chichester*, UK) – Gerald O. West (*University of KwaZulu-Natal, South Africa*) – Andrew Wilson (*Mount Allison University, Canada*) – Caroline Vander Stichele (*University of Amsterdam, Netherlands*)

Volumes published in this Brill Research Perspectives title are listed at *brill.com/rpbi*

The Sense of Quoting

A Semiotic Case Study of Biblical Quotations

By

David W. Odell-Scott

BRILL

LEIDEN | BOSTON

This paperback book edition is simultaneously published as issue 2.4 (2017) of *Biblical Interpretation*, DOI 10.1163/24057657-12340010.

The Library of Congress Cataloging-in-Publication Data is available online at http://catalog.loc.gov

Typeface for the Latin, Greek, and Cyrillic scripts: "Brill". See and download: brill.com/brill-typeface.

ISBN 978-90-04-36193-5 (paperback)
ISBN 978-90-04-36194-2 (e-book)

Copyright 2017 by David W. Odell-Scott. Published by Koninklijke Brill NV, Leiden, The Netherlands.
Koninklijke Brill NV incorporates the imprints Brill, Brill Hes & De Graaf, Brill Nijhoff, Brill Rodopi, Brill Sense and Hotei Publishing.
Koninklijke Brill NV reserves the right to protect the publication against unauthorized use and to authorize dissemination by means of offprints, legitimate photocopies, microform editions, reprints, translations, and secondary information sources, such as abstracting and indexing services including databases. Requests for commercial re-use, use of parts of the publication, and/or translations must be addressed to Koninklijke Brill NV.

This book is printed on acid-free paper and produced in a sustainable manner.

Contents

The Sense of Quoting
A Semiotic Case Study of Biblical Quotations   1
      David W. Odell-Scott
  Abstract   1
  Keywords   1
  Part 1. Introduction   2
      Semiotic Analysis of Discursive Texts   9
  Part 2. On Quoting   13
      Writing, Reading and Scoring the Continuous Script(ure)   17
          Elementary Reading of Continuous Script   21
          Sentences and Quotations   26
      Textual Cohesiveness and Semiotics Textus   28
          Punctuation as Technique and Technology for Contextualizing a Script   31
      Features and Factors   39
      Conclusion   46
  Part 3. Manufacturing Plainer Passages   50
      Orthodox Quotations: Augustine on Sentential Order   50
      Quoting a Quote and the Question of a Plainer Passage   58
          The Case of Male Celibacy   58
          Re-scored Standard Rendition of Extended Script 1 Cor 7:1–6   69
          Rescored Alternative Rendition of Extended Script 1 Cor 7:1–6   70
      Concluding the Question of Plainer Passages: Augustine and the Persistence of Semiotic Issues   75
      Concluding Considerations   79
          Pragmatics   79
          Post-Script   81
  Works Cited   85

The Sense of Quoting
A Semiotic Case Study of Biblical Quotations

David W. Odell-Scott
Kent State University, USA
dodellsc@kent.edu

Abstract

This essay argues that the neutral continuous script of ancient manuscripts of the Greek New Testament composed with no punctuation and no spacing provided readers discretionary authority to determine and assess the status of phrases as they articulated a cohesive and coherent reading of the script. The variety of reading renditions, each differently scored with punctuation, supported the production of quotations. These cultivated and harvested quotes, while useful for authorizing sectarian discourse, rarely convey the sense of the phrase in the continuous script. Augustine's work on punctuating the scriptures in service to the production of plainer quotable passages in support of the rule of faith is addressed. The textual analysis of a plainer quotable passage at 1 Cor. 7:1b concerning male celibacy supports the thesis that plainer passages are the product of interpretative scoring of the script in service to discursive endeavours. To quote is often to misquote.

Keywords

quotations – celibacy – Paul – Greek New Testament – semiotics – discourse analysis – punctuation

Part 1. Introduction

ΠΕΡΙΔΕΩΝΕΓΡΑΨΑΤΕ
ΚΑΛΟΝΑΝΘΡΩΠΩΓΥ
ΝΑΙΚΟϹΜΗΑΠΤΕϹΘΑΙ
ΔΙΑΔΕΤΑϹΠΟΡΝΙΑϹ
ΕΚΑϹΤΟϹΤΗΝΕΑΥΤΟΥ
ΓΥΝΑΙΚΑΕΧΕΤΩΚΑΙΕ
ΚΑϹΤΗΤΟΝΪΔΙΟΝΑΝ
ΔΡΑΕΧΕΤΩΤΗΓΥΝΑΙ
ΚΙΟΑΝΗΡΤΗΝΟΦΙΛΗΝ
ΑΠΟΔΙΔΟΤΩΟΜΟΙΩϹ
ΔΕΚΑΙΗΓΥΝΗΤΩΑΔΡΙ
ΗΓΥΝΗΤΟΥΪΔΙΟΥϹΩ
ΜΑΤΟϹΟΥΚΕΞΟΥϹΙΑΖΕΙ
ΑΛΛΑΟΑΝΗΡΟΜΟΙΩϹ
ΔΕΚΑΙΟΑΝΗΡΤΟΥΪΔΙ

ΟΥϹΩΜΑΤΟϹΟΥΚΕΞΟΥ
ϹΙΑΖΕΙΑΛΛΑΗΓΥΝΗΜΗ
ΑΠΟϹΤΕΡΙΤΕΑΛΛΗΛΟΥϹ
ΕΙΜΗΤΙΕΚϹΥΜΦΩΝΟΥ
ΠΡΟϹΚΑΙΡΟΝΙΝΑϹΧΟ
ΛΑϹΗΤΕΤΗΠΡΟϹΕΥΧΗ
ΚΑΙΠΑΛΙΝΕΠΙΤΟΑΥΤΟ
ΗΤΕΙΝΑΜΗΠΙΡΑΖΗΫ
ΜΑϹΟϹΑΤΑΝΑϹΔΙΑΤΗ
ΑΚΡΑϹΙΑΤΟΥΤΟΔΕΛΕ
ΓΩΚΑΤΑϹΥΓΓΝΩΜΗΝ[1]

1 COR 7:1–6

M. B. Parkes characterized the *scriptio continua* of Ancient, Hellenistic and Medieval Greek manuscripts as "neutral" (Parkes 1992, 11). The characterization of neutrality is based on the manuscripts having been written without the features of punctuation and spacing between words, and in all capital letters. Sentential order made evident by punctuation was administered at the discretion of a reader. The production of Greek manuscripts of the New Testament appointed with punctuation and spatially styled were rare well towards the end of the first millennium of the Common Era.

I argue that the desire and design for sentential order in the manuscripts of Christian scriptures were motivated in part by the competitions among the plurality of competing if not contesting Christian movements. Each pursued their own reading and interpretation of the text with each drawing out their own quotations of scripture in support of their sectarian communal convictions and practices. The "scoring" of the "neutral script" by means of the use

---

[1] This transcription is produced from a photo of Codex 02, otherwise known as Codex Vaticanus. The left column begins with 1 Corinthians 7:1 and proceeds to the end of the column on the right with verse 6. In the manuscript, chapter 7 begins 2/3 down the left side column and transitions to the top of the center column. In the photo of the codex it is apparent that at some later point (some argue as late as eight centuries following the production of the codex) Arabic chapter and verse numbers were added in the left margin of each column.

of marks of punctuation served to support a reader's preferred reading of the scripture through the use of the period to distinguish one phrase from another. Such non-alphabetical markings served to establish clarity as to sentential units drawn by parsing the continuous script. But such parsing of the continuous script was not a "neutral" affair.

I offer the term "scoring" of biblical manuscripts as a play upon the sense of inscribing graphic non-alphabetical markings which like features in a musical score are to be factored into the grammar and reading performance of the work. To sight read a sheet of music is to review how to give a first read of a piece. But the technical challenges often do not appear on a first read as the complexities often emerge only as one plays through and thoroughly begins to engage the textures woven into a work. Complex works require multiple readings and reading performances to discern often important subtle details which emerge only in playing through and with the text. Thus, to "score" a textual work of music is to convey features which inform the interplay of reading, performance and musical grammar. "Re-scoring" a piece, as in the reading performer inscribing notations which express and serve to influence the reading and performance is to offer a *rendition* which render changes concerning the tempo, key, articulations, emphasis, differentiations in volume and various modulations of the work.

Such "scoring" of the "neutral" script of the manuscripts of the New Testament were undertaken to influence different renditions of the script in a reading performance. I argue that how the script was read under the influence of a rendition so marked with punctuation served to support a reading. The punctuation marks served to inscribe a reading rendition into the text. A specific reading rendition could support or foreclose the production of specific quotations to be drawn out of the Christian scriptures concerning the faithful convictions and practices of a sectarian legacy. Thus, choices in scoring the neutral script could bespeak one's own preferences for how to read and which phrases to emphasize in service to their harvesting phrases so scored as quotations, or serve to foreclose the preferences of another's reading and the harvesting of their valued quotations.

Part One of the essay concerns two semiotic mechanisms of quoting scripture. The first concerns the production of quotes from the Bible. The second mechanism is the sense or presence of a phrase as a quotation incorporated in a scriptural text. The characteristic proffered by Parkes that the texts as composed *scriptio continua* are "neutral" serves to highlight that the selection of a phrase for quoting and the selection of a phrase as a quotation in the script may be at the discretion of the reader influenced by the interplay of the written language of the script and the sense of the reading of the script as performed by the reader. On Parkes's evaluation, the neutral continuous script was unencumbered and thus free to be parsed and performed by the reader. The scoring of the neutral script by readers over time influenced by the emergent systems and codes of punctuation and style later came to be traced into the productions of manuscripts.

However, towards the conclusion of Part One I return to critically reconsider Parkes's assessment that the *scriptio continua* features of the manuscripts of Christian scripture were "neutral." I argue that Parkes's analysis and assessment while valuable and useful is limited by the perspective he takes up regarding the Greek continuous script in relation to the "refinement" and "development" of a "repertory" of non-alphabetical features of punctuation rendered in the production of non-neutral scored medieval manuscripts and modern print productions. That is, neutrality is an assessment which assumes a perspective based on the complex productions of manufacturing the script for sectarian purposes with the use of non-alphabetical graphic marks and the manufacturing of stylized spacing in the structuring of the script. I contend that such a perspective shows little regard or concern for an analysis of the semiotic and semantic constructions at work in the production of the Greek texts which served to "score" the continuous script. Further, I argue that the evolution and use of punctuation to score the script for sectarian purposes, served to overlay or better, cover over or up the ancient existing Greek "scoring" features incorporated in the earlier rendering of the script in transcription.

I proffer that Parkes's "neutral" continuous script argument, while heuristically valuable for reasons which will become evident as we progress, is nevertheless mistaken if not forthrightly wrong as concerns the "neutrality" of ancient Greek manuscripts of the New Testament. To usher us into this consideration, I offer the following observation and assessment by Ludwig Wittgenstein in his *Philosophical Investigations*.

> Imagine a script in which the letters were used to stand for sounds, and also as signs of emphasis and punctuation. (A script may be conceived as a language for describing sound-patterns.) Now imagine someone interpreting that script as if there were simply a correspondence of letters to sounds and as if the letters had not also completely different functions. Augustine's conception of language is like such an over-simple conception of the script.
>   WITTGENSTEIN 2001, P. 3^e. #4

Suppose that the Greek continuous script of the New Testament manuscripts, and earlier the script as produced at the hand of the transcriber, were embedded with Greek letters which did not "correspond" to words or the sounds of words but supplied information as signs which served to note "emphasis and punctuation" (on Wittgenstein's terms). For Wittgenstein punctuation includes the markings of regular written language and certainly the punctuation of logical arguments. In the *Tractatus Logico-Philosophicus* he writes, "Signs for logical operations are punctuation-marks" (Wittgenstein 1961, 5.4611). Could there be such letter signs embedded in the continuous Greek scripts of the manuscripts of the New Testament, which are signs of emphasis and punctuation but that do not correspond to sounds of words or words proper? And that given the privilege to spelled out word-signs in the script (Wittgenstein's critical point concerning Augustine), the letters which did not spell out word-signs in the script but served to *note* emphasis and punctuation, so in some cases produce sounds of emphasis and punctuation, pass unread and unnoticed in plain sight, or at least glossed over? Or, if translated as contributing to spelled out word-signs, would such a reading be so much a misreading of the script that as Wittgenstein goes on to note, such reading of a script would produce gibberish based on a confusion as to the sense and purpose of the lettered marks concerning other operations in the script? Are there such markings hidden in plain sight in the Greek New Testament? And do such lettered features convey information concerning how the words and phrasing of the text (also spelled out with letters) are to be emphasized, signs which inform how the phrases and larger units articulate in the script in generating textual cohesiveness by means of connectivity informed by Greek letter-signs, thus informing the conceptual connectivity of the script (De Beaugrande 1980, 10)?

I sought the advice of a respected New Testament scholar on an early draft of my article on 1 Corinthians 14:34–36 while a doctoral student in philosophy, an article in which I made much of the significance of the Greek negative particle η (eta) in conveying how the script was structured as a "letter" in which Paul quoted the Corinthians (verses 34 & 35) in order to forthrightly and directly pivot beginning at verse 36 with the η in issuing a twofold negative rhetorical reply (Odell-Scott 1991, 190). I was told very directly that my concern with the influence of a Greek "particle" in the script was ill advised. He declared forcefully that the particles are nothing: they mean nothing. I pointed out in reply "why are there so many particles at such important sites in Paul's letters to the Corinthians?" I was met with dismissal. Being dismissed, I retreated to the library and in an afternoon discovered a variety of substantive works which addressed the often-ignored use of Greek particles in ancient manuscripts (Dennison). The judgment that "they (particles) mean nothing" suggested yet again at the time the continued influence of Augustine's abridged Aristotelian semiotics even by a scholar who championed an historic critical method.

Greek particles are commonly defined by grammarians as expressing the interrelations of sentences and clauses, and also in giving greater prominence to the modal character of a clause or sentence (Blass, Debrunner and Funk 1961, 225). Whether composed of one or several Greek letters—as regards the continuous script—particles supply information as to the status of a phrase, the cohesiveness and articulations of a script which produces by means of the processes of reading a continuous Greek script an understanding of a work as a conceptual coherent *textus*. And it is the case that the non-alphabetical graphic markings of "punctuation" added to the composition by readers, editors, copyist and publishers scoring the text, supply information expressing the interrelations of sentences and clauses, and serve in giving prominence to the modal character of a clause or sentence of a written manuscript or printed modern text. But particles transcribed in an ancient Greek manuscript and punctuation added by subsequent readers are not equivalent. I contend that what has transpired is that the function of particles under operational codes and conventions in Ancient and Hellenic Greek writing and reading in continuous script slowly faded in consideration by readers almost to the point of being found to contribute little if nothing to the understanding of the text. And this drift, this fading of the influence of the particles happened in tandem as the different operational codes and conventions of emergent systems of punctuation to demarcate a phrase and the status of a phrase, and so to note the cohesiveness and articulations of a script came to support other means of rendering the script a coherent text. Thus, in concert with this exchange of operational codes and conventions, I would not argue as to the causation of the obsolescence of particles and their operational codes as the dominant mechanisms for "scoring" a continuous script. The nascent alternative operational codes and conventions of punctuation, evolved over the centuries through medieval manuscript production, writing and reading, and attained a predominant function as the means for "scoring" in modern writing, publishing and reading following the invention and establishment of machine printing. The drift from one semiotic system employed to score or mark a composed *textus* in association with changes in the scoring and mastery of writing from continuous script to styled spacing of words, sentences, paragraphs and larger units of text, and from all capital lettering to the differentiations of function for lower and upper-case lettering, and the resultant scoring methods eventually incorporated in the composition and production of a work stretched over more than a millennium. As to the causes or reasons for these changes in writing and reading, for the differences and developments in scoring and noting the status and completeness of phrases and sentences, and for manifesting in the script the plays of cohesiveness, coherence and articulations, such an epic project is clearly beyond the limits of this short essay.

My use of Wittgenstein's comments is a means to segue into the conversations about the complexities and foreignness of composing and reading ancient Greek manuscripts, and to usher into the conversation the evidence that Greek particles operated in "scoring" the script such that contra Parkes's assessment concerning neutrality, the ancient Greek manuscripts were always already robustly appointed.

In Part II. I begin with a consideration of Augustine's *De Doctrina Christina* (*On Christian Teaching*) in which he addresses the complications which arise when dealing with what he assesses to be an ambiguous passage or sentence in the continuous script of the New Testament. He takes issue with those who deploy "punctuation" or offer a rendition in their reading performance of a scripture text which so appointed or performed as to produce a sense of the work which supports the potential for the drawing out of quotations which fail to support or may even challenge the rule of faith. I critically examine Augustine's insistence on what he assesses are "plainer passages" which he argues serve in the adjudication on how to resolve conflicts over reading, appointing and performing ambiguous passages. His strategy is to employ the "plainer passages" such that the resulting clarity provided in a reading supports an orthodox rule of faith. I focus in on a passage which Augustine employs in the corpus of his works to be one of the plainer passages: "It is good for a man not to touch a woman." The much-quoted declaration attributed to Paul is quoted from the seventh chapter of 1 Corinthians. I introduced the quoted verse as it occurs in the Greek continuous script at the head of this Introduction to the essay. I argue contra Augustine, that the status of the verse as *plainer* is a product of a manipulation and manufacturing of the script with the techniques of scoring by the addition of punctuation into the larger continuous script. The larger text is so scored that a reading is produced which highlights the phrase as a useful quotation in support of an institutional discourse thus establishing the propriety of a celibate all male clergy in the Christian churches. I argue that the continuous script serves as a resource for manipulation and manufacturing in the production of the preferred reading and valued quotations in service to the religious socio-political actions, plans and goals of orthodox Christian churches. Nevertheless, there are complications with the manufactured sentential order of the larger text in which the quote is a phrase. The complication is that the manufactured production of the plainer passage and the sentential ordering of the larger passage fails to adequately take into consideration the status of the phrasing of the script and the implications of the use of particles in considering how the script is cohesive, and articulates a coherent *textus*. And of course, the manufactured plainer phrase from the *scriptio continua* will be found to have failed to take into consideration at the most elementary level the introduction of the phrase as a quotation which Paul draws from something written to him from the Corinthian church. The phrase so rendered as a plainer passage as presenting Paul's position, is complicated if not compromised because the phrase is a quotation which defenders of male celibacy liberally quote as Paul's position without hesitation as to the purpose of Paul's quoting the declaration from the Corinthians. What is ambiguous, what complicates the assessment of the phrase as a plainer presentation of Paul's position, is that the status of the phrase as a quotation drawn by Paul into his larger discursive missive to the Corinthians was to quote a phrase they addressed to him for his consideration and to which he replied.

What if the phrase quoted by Paul was incorporated into his reply to the Corinthians not to support their claim, but to serve as the target for his critique? I argue that the common classical reading of the phrase "It is good for a man not to touch a woman" as a plainer presentation of Paul's position fails to take into account several rudimentary features of the Greek text. The play of particles in the script of an epistle may serve as significant textual features to give greater prominence to the modal character (Blass, Debrunner and Funk 1961, 225). Hurd notes that "while δε occurs several times at the turning points of 1 Corinthians, it usually carries an adversative sense" (Hurd 1965, 90, fn. 2). In such identified junctures in the epistle, the author may be taking an adversative posture to positions maintained by the party to whom the letter is addressed. Thus, the "joint or cut" in the script does not mark the end of one discourse and the beginning of another (Odell-Scott 1991, 174). Rather, the junction concerns an engagement, a critical engagement by the author with the phrases quoted. I argue that the connectivity of the phrase "It is good for a man not to touch a woman" to the introduction and to what follows, is complicated by syntactical and semantic features of the *textus*, evident as well in the use of the particle δε which is often not acknowledged in the rush to identify the phrase as a plainer proclamation of Paul's position for purposes of sectarian quoting. I propose other readings of the script which consider Paul's quoting "a matter about which you wrote" that highlights features evident in the script but ignored in the classical reading. My proposed alternative rendering of the script with attention to the use and placement of particles, especially the particle δε in conjunction with other features serve to influence a different reading renditions of the larger text as articulating a different textual cohesive reading of the script as a adversative engagement. An alternative rendition draws upon features of the Greek syntax and semantics that attends to the use of Greek particles, and considers pragmatic elements concerning the status of the quoted phrase as occasioning Paul's direct and coherent critique in reply to "The matter which you wrote: 'it is good for a man not to touch a woman.'"

Semiotic Analysis of Discursive Texts

To aid in the analysis of the interplay of the production of biblical quotes for sectarian Christian discursive purposes and the endeavors to manufacture sentential order upon and in the continuous script, I draw upon a variety of interrelated semiotic approaches concerning what is broadly identified as discourse analysis, which is also referred to as text analysis, text linguistics, and text semiotics. My preference is semiotic *textus* or *textus* semiotics for reasons which I offer later. The selection of terms like "discourse," "text" or "*textus*" as what is to be analyzed serves to differentiate "discourse" or "text" from the smaller units of speech or writing which are incorporated into the larger context of presentation or text of a discourse. The second though closely related semiotic approach I employ analyses the associations of a discourse or text with social and political advocacy (or as expressive of the naturalized discourse which serves institutional ideology). Thus, critical discourse analysis and discourse analysis are interactive approaches as each provides insight and information to be considered in an analysis of discourse.

Stanley Porter notes the difficulties in defining discourse analysis. For while the three areas of Peircean semiotics which inform linguistic analysis are formulated to address such basic interrelated functions as semantics, syntax and pragmatics in the study of texts, what remains a hallmark of discourse analysis is the persistent attention paid to how smaller meaningful units of language are incorporated into larger discursive units which articulate cohesiveness in the composition of meaningful units writ large, at levels greater than that of a sentence if not at the level of a text as a whole. Such weaving of smaller language units in the composition of a text concerns the interaction among micro- and macro-structures in which the sense of any part writ large or small influences and is influenced by the progressive contextual articulations of a cohesive whole (Porter 1995, 19). An analysis of a discursive text involves a consideration of how textual coherence is produced by means of the cohesiveness provided in informational structures (such as lexical choice), prominence, linguistic co-text and context.

Language is regarded as a social-semiotic instrument or tool that operates in communication and social interaction in discourse analysis approaches. (Porter 1995, 20). The early development of the critical discourse analysis approach according to de Beaugrande understood such analysis as "text grammar" or as Porter puts it "the methods used were essentially an extension of sentence grammars ..." (Porter 1995, 19–20). However, the classical preoccupation with sentential structures as the unit for analysis was found to be inadequate when considering how a text so weaves language in a cohesive and coherent articulation writ large. The classical operative grammar assumed an ontology which served to construct isolated individual sentence units thus too often foreclosing the analysis of larger operations that incorporated multiple discreet sentences into complex cohesive articulating discourses. In discourse analysis the status and meaning of a specific sentence unit was found to be dependent upon the cohesive articulations between phrases and sentences in a textured discourse. Thus, the contextualization of a sentence for analysis as a unit embedded and dependent upon a text writ large considers such smaller units which articulate in a discursive cohesiveness in which sentences are more than a collection of autonomous sentential units. To repeat, albeit twisted, a collection of autonomous sentences does not a text make. The characteristic of a text is that the sentences so interact that together in the textured cohesive articulations a coherence which exceeds the individual parts is produced by the reading. The question arose early in modern critical semiotic theory as to the site or cause of such cohesive articulating coherence to be found in the event or object or artifact or system under consideration. The semiotic approaches generally regard simple resolutions that the source of such features was borne of the subject doing the inquiry, the object being studied, the language which conveyed the information from subject to object or object to subject, let alone the tools of inquiry including the identification of pertinent factors, as all being inadequate. Piercing semiotic approaches relied upon triadic interactions without simple foundations (epistemic or metaphysical) to vouch safe the engagements. For Peirce there are three general categories of signification for signs. "Sign vehicles signify by virtue of qualities, existential (physical) facts, or conventions (habits, or laws)" (Odell-Scott & Aichele 2013, 2, 288).

De Beaugrande argued that "The text is an actual system, while sentences are elements of a virtual system ..." (De Beaugrande 11). I take that one of his points is that a characteristic of a sentence is its potentiality which is actualized in a textual system. Thus a phrase without context exhibits potentiality as a virtual system which may be differently actualized in different actual text systems. Thus given the topic of this essay concerning quoting, a sentence or phrase embedded in a text may in context be actualized and serve to make the sense of the phrase or sentence more or less determined. However, the processes of identifying a phrase or sentence as having "potential" as a quote harvested from an actual text, releases the sense of the phrase from its actualized context. The potential of a quotation bespeaks the status of sentences and phrases as elements of a virtual system, "open" for a variety of potentially different deployments in other actualizing texts. So released the phrase or sentence as quoted is available to be actualized differently in a subsequent discursive text. Of course once the phrase or sentence is re-contextualized the sense of the quote is settled or determined as a quote in the discursive text. A text becomes "a functional unity created through processes of decision and selection among options of virtual systems" (De Beaugrande 1980, 16).

But what is to be made of an actual system (a text) when a contributing feature such as a Greek particle and its operational codes and conventions fade from use in the teaching, art and act of reading a biblical script? What actuality of a text is forgotten as the Greek particles recede from view and their contributions to how the script actualizes cohesiveness, articulations and coherence fade in supplying operational information when reading? De Beaugrande writes that "The sentence is a purely grammatical entity to be defined only on the level of syntax. The text must be defined according to the complete standards of textuality ..." (De Beaugrande 1980, 12). But what are we to consider when the operational systems which inform the "complete standards" of textuality concerning an ancient Greek biblical manuscript, have been amended in an ongoing protracted history whereby the "text" is rescored such that one set of markers for determining status, cohesiveness, coherence and articulations of phrases and sentences are superimposed into the script and serve in some sense to displace if not compromise or even confuse the contributions of the operational systems which inform the uses of particles as regards the "complete standards" of textuality when reading a continuous Greek script?

Conceptions of textuality in discourse analysis are somewhat stressed when we consider that an Ancient Greek manuscript such as a work included in the anthology of the New Testament was composed in continuous script without the notion that the text was the result of the cohesiveness of autonomous sentences composed like parts into a constructed composition. The complication comes when the continuous script is aided in its articulations not by the presence of autonomous sentences which are actualized by means of the use of punctuation and style into a coherent cohesive actual system/text. Rather, the continuous script operates as a process of sequential connectivity (syntax) such that lines or threads of conceptual connectivity serve in their associations to occasion an emergent actual sense of a text from which the production of autonomous sentences were drawn.

"When elements of a presented text are forgotten, the textual system in mental storage adjusts by compacting, rearranging, or reconstructing the remainder" (De Beaugrande 1980, 18). De Beaugrande's conception of "mental storage" concerns the functional recall and use of a text, which on his terms is a reconstructed text drawn from the *remainder* of the text remembered minus the forgotten elements. There are two points to be made in preparation for the study to follow related to this point. First, when the reading and meaning of a text produced with elements or features that contributed to the "complete standards" of the textual operation are no longer taught or acknowledged or understood by subsequent readers, the result is that readers proceed as if in the dark as to what signs mean in a text. Having lost what elements or features to consider readers proceed by compacting, rearranging and reconstructing the text unaware of the very features which serve as signs for syntax, semantics and pragmatic information. Second, quoting a text whereby a textual system is harvested for bits and pieces which are compacted, rearranged and reconstructed in a subsequent discourse, is to forget or possibly to ignore the full *textus* of the source of such harvesting for the sake of production and the satisfaction of one's aspirations for the composition of a successful discourse.

The history of Christianity may be characterized by the fact that few persons possessed the requisite skills to read the gospel aloud to themselves or to an audience, whether in Greek or translation, prior to the achievements of modern print production and the modern campaigns for universal literacy. I would venture that acquaintance with Christian scriptures (in Greek or translation) for most persons prior to modernity was piecemeal, as the works were fragmented into manageable sentential units as quotations drawn by others who could read. And these quotations were heard and known as they were performed in the discursive life of ecclesiastical institutions, and as employed by being repeated in conversation. Without the benefit of reading texts for themselves, the vast non-reading public would be vulnerable to those who could read and who fashioned quotations from scripture in service to their discourse. Such an economy of advantage and disadvantage runs through the history in most reading and use of scripture. And depending on the intellect and memory of the listening public who could not read, and the extent of their experiences of the texts through oral performance delivered by others, such listening persons might not catch the complication posed by the selection of a quote from say the Gospel of Matthew wherein Jesus declared "Love your neighbor and hate your enemy." For without the skill of reading the text for one's self, without access to a manuscript, or lacking opportunity, time and curiosity, one might find credence in the quotation declared by another that Jesus said "hate your enemy." Without the requisite knowledge of the text, drawn together at least second hand from another who could read, the features indicating that the quoted phrase was presented in the script as an adversarial position (so emphasized by the presence of the particle δε) as quoted by Jesus to stage Jesus declaring his counter teaching "Love your enemy and pray for those who persecute you" would be forgotten (Matthew 5: 43–44). For the reader performing the text might so emphasize the phrase as a quote giving it prominence in the production of a coherent and cohesive discourse that the phrase supported loving your neighbor and hating your enemy could be received as a valued social and political conviction championed in scripture by Jesus. Thus, at play in this brief and apparently simple example, are the interactions of semantics, syntax and pragmatics in the life of a phrase, in which an actualized text was harvested for a virtual quotable sentence that could be reconstructed.

Part 2. On Quoting

To quote is to repeat. To repeat a phrase may be to say or to write again, what one heard or what one read. To quote the bible is to re-say or re-write a phrase which one read or heard another read aloud or to repeat from memory. To quote another who from memory re-said or re-wrote a phrase from Christian scripture in their religious practice, formal discourse or even informal conversation is to participate in a semiotic rich production of scripture in Christian life. In the repetitive saying and writing of phrases from scripture in all manner of Christian discursive life, the quoted bits of the scripture are fashioned to say and write "more" if not "other" in being re-said and re-written in other contexts post-scripture. That is, the quoting of phrases from the New Testament in social commerce and exchange is a post-script production that correlates and distributes scripture in inscriptive engagements. I contend that to a considerable extent, knowledge of Christian scriptures comes to us by bits and phrases in the functional discursive repeating of quotations that correlate quoted phrases in often-vibrant inscriptive engagements. Such functional quoting of scripture serves to recycle the repeated phrases and such recycling through all manner of saying and writing serves to re-task the scriptural phrases in contexts for "more" and "other" purposes. Thus, in being repeated in bits and phrases in discursive re-sayings and rewritings, in saying and writing "more" or "other" through recycling and re-tasking, the functional sense of such quoting informs divergent meaningful associations and correlations with the source text from which the phrases were drawn in different "pragmatic" contexts.

To quote, as in to repeat, is an elementary though complex cognitive or neurological function of presenting what was heard or what was read. To repeat is a presentation that seeks in some sense to represent. To repeat a birdcall or song is to mimic. If one can reproduce the call of a night owl, a call which mimics the qualities of tone, melody, timing, and volume all of which modulate and articulate, one might attract the specific owl to fly in up out of the wooded hollow into the large oak out back of the parsonage. Moreover, for a time, we engage in an elementary play of call and repeat, with subtle modulations and articulations introduced by both myself and the owl and quoted back in our exchange such that the song minutely changes in the course of the event before the bard owl returns to its woods down in the hollow and I to my study. What counts as our signals or signatures are unclear beyond some elementary level of significance associated with the birdsong, both his and mine. Such repeating, such quoting, such mimicking play out interesting communication which in this example is limited in terms of conceptual content being that the specific bard owl and I would call and repeat in our late night venture correlated in some vague elementary sense as very ambiguous cross species signals or signatures. For me, it signaled a specific bard owl whose call differed from the calls of others I heard in the woods and who was the one who would fly and perch in the same tree though unseen in the deep dark of a rural night out our back door. It also suggested that our repeating the specific birdcall served to attract us both on occasion when in the still of the night we entered into our mimetic endeavor. I do not want to make more of this example other than to suggest that "quoting" is a mimetic activity that may play upon elementary cognitive functions that do little more than exhibit simple ambiguous signals that signify little more than a vague signature. Or play in some sense to cohesively sequence by means of catch phrase. As such, in some rudimentary sense quoting-repeating are basic epistemic processes (Foucault sense) given that in such instances we share what counts as evidence for our signals or signatures.

Biblical quotations, drawn out, harvested and employed in the production of Christian discursive ventures, deployed in social and political engagements often serve to signal belonging to one's own in opposition with other contending persons, parties, churches and movements. Such quotations and the discourses in which they operate are among the paramount artifacts that operate under the sway of specific Christian cultures. These cultural artifacts are archived in the historic Christian social and political institutions. To archive the discursive ventures of Christian influence in historic social and political institutions, even in the nascent emergence of Christian societies or in complex often-inchoate discursive play as if in foreign if not hostile contexts, is to identify and explain scriptural quotes as epistemic artifacts. They count for ways of knowing.

Tooling the scripture by harvesting a selected phrase for repeating means that the valued phrase is figuratively cut out of the text by means of abstracting the phrase from a source for repeating. This production is less figurative when the valued phrase is rewritten, copied for future deployment or copied into a discursive venture. This production of creating quotes from the manuscripts of scripture in the early centuries of the first millennium were likened to a reader cutting out the desired phrase to be quoted from the undifferentiated continuous script. Phrases so harvested are referred to in ecclesiastical circles as pericopes. The Greek term περικοπη from περι "around" and κοπη as in "cutting" suggests that a phrase so prepared is "cut round" so as to be "cut out" of the script (much like cutting with a coping saw). It is suggested that in some instances the work of such "cutting" results in the mutilation of the site from which the quote was harvested. In such instance, the "site" is trashed in the production of the desired phrase for quoting. A text so harvested is reduced to debris as the desired quote so cut out renders the text as little more than the waste product of manufacturing.

In a significant way when a harvested quote is integrated and so inhabits a successful discourse the sense bequeathed to the quote in such discursive habitation becomes the effective meaning of the quoted phrase. And when the dominant forces of Christian political, social and cultural institutions reinforce the discursive framing of the quoted phrase, and the discourse correlates in the associated institutional structures, the sense of the quote as determined in the discursive correlation functions as if it were "natural." The successful incorporation of a pericope into ecclesiastical instituted discourse serves by means of its habitation in the shared correlations to determine the meaning and context of the quoted phrase in the life of a community. The power of the historical situation and the pervasive influence of the cultural and social discourse come to exercise an energy (an ενεργια as in to actualize a potential) which is determinative of the meaning of the phrase. And this actualization of the sense of the quote migrates when the phrase is read again in the source text from which the phrase was harvested.

The persuasive energy of quoting scripture for Christian discursive purposes is such that so long and to the extent to which the framing discourse persist to persuade, so long as the discursive use of the quote is correlated with the life of an individual and the life of a community, then the quote is activated and operationalized under the persuasive energy of the discourse. Such a quotation serves in the discourse as a "token," as standing for the source. The quoted phrase in the context of the instituted discourse thus usurps the content and draws upon the authority of the scripture text (and attributed author) from which a pericope was harvested. As if under the manipulation of a conjurer, the successful orator quotes the pericope whether in liturgical performance, proclamations or teaching and so transforms the quote such that the content, status and meaning of the quoted phrase even when read in the source script often comes to be determined by the discursive frame in which the quote operates.

Classical rhetoric began primarily as a system for training young men in families with position in the art of eloquent and persuasive public speaking to support their political and social aspirations in the institutions of participatory democracy. The ability to persuade others of the rightness of one's cause or case, or by the power of an eloquent discourse to bind others to join in one's endeavors was a means for achievement in all quarters and at most levels of democratic societies. One of the admired techniques for demonstrating oratory or authorial eloquence was through the mastery of drawn quotations from the classics, popular literature and essays of the day in one's own public addresses, debates or written work. The execution of well-crafted *sententiae*, those memorable maxims, proverbs and aphorism drawn from an authoritative or respected source served to command the attention and respect of the literate elite who figured prominently in the halls of government, the courts and public opinion. Much was made of a properly rhetorically trained reader who would compile and order their borrowed *sententiae* as "quotable quotes" by topics for quick reference when composing a speech, preparing for a debate or presenting a case in court (see *Sententiae*, chapter 2, in Quintilian's *Institutio Oratoria*). The quality of a selected quotation and the art of eloquent use in presentation for maximum effect was much valued.

In antiquity, when it comes to quoting another in oration, it was common practice to incorporate a quote without formally introducing the quote. It was assumed among those schooled in the arts of rhetoric and oration that drawing upon a shared body of works it was the responsibility of the audience to exhibit their good learning by individually knowing a quote, the source and author. To not know a quotation or an allusion to a work as a member of the audience listening to an eloquent orator was for a member of an audience to be found wanting. It was not the responsibility of the orator to cite and introduce his sources. Of course, a truly eloquent performance could perform the quote such that the presence of a quotation would be indicated by the nuances of delivery, a change of tone or pace or pause. A persuasive orator would skillfully draw upon works and quotations that were part of the common stock of known *sententiae* familiar among the educated elite.

The use of quotations drawn by an elite orator in Greco-Roman society, provided a means for the manipulation of works with authority by those who already enjoyed the privileges of their station in society that they exercised as readers in a society in which the majority were illiterate. Those who drew quotations (Latin *sententiae* or Greek περικοπη) did so from an advantage given that as literate members of the elite there was little means for those who were illiterate to examine the text from which the quote was drawn. Thus, without the checks and balances provided by a broad-based literate society, those with authority could draw upon authoritative texts with little oversight as to the quality of the identification and selection of the phrase as presenting are representing the source work. Questions as to the cohesiveness and coherence of a source text to support the viability and integrity of a selected quote was not common practice.

In the broadest sense Christian societies, cultures, institutions and life are saturated with borrowed materials from the scriptures. Some of the material drawn is clear-cut pericope of short phrases, whole sentences or multi-sentence extended verses. Other "borrowing" includes paraphrases and reminiscences if not allusions.

Quotations inform institutional structure and influence what it means to live a faithful life. Such drawing and use of quotations often enrich symbolic and ritual action, and punctuate convictional discourse adding content to belief or an argument. Such quoting is oft employed so as to deliver an effect upon the reader or an audience at a public reading. Biblical quotations matter in the rich array of Christian discourse.

Biblical quoting is common among all contending parties who seek to forward their influence within and among Christian societies, institutions and cultures. Despite characteristic differences within various movements and ecclesial institutions that compete with one another, all competitors share more or less in common the functional harvesting of biblical quotes and the deploying of such phrases as quotations to legitimate their authority and to enhance the privilege of their specific discursive legacy. Nevertheless, differences between the competitive movements and ecclesial institutions are manifest as regards which phrases are harvested, for what purpose their quote is deployed or applied, the discourse in which the quote functions, as well as the social and political contexts in which such quotes occur. Yet, in competitive situations, quotations are deployed as if they are weapons of battle. For inter-Christian battles over all manner of topics is commonly waged with the strategic deployment of drawn biblical quotations. Such quotations often serve as tactical weapons. The effort to succeed is to attain dominance and to so enjoy the prestige and proprieties of the faith. Such battles of the quotes are the inter-Christian fields of conceptual, symbolic and convictional war.

Writing, Reading and Scoring the Continuous Script(ure)

The influence of classical rhetoric in the development of classical Christian writing and oration is complicated by if not fostered by the material cultures of writing and reading in the centuries before and following the ministry of Jesus. Ancient Greek and Latin manuscripts were written and copied in dense lines of all capital letters in a continuous script. Further, the continuous script, dense with each line composed one letter immediately after the other without spacing to set words apart, were also composed without the use of non-alphabetical graphic markings of punctuation. The techniques of spacing and punctuating manuscripts, and the codes and conventions that informed and supported their use and function in writing and reading, had yet to be invented let alone operationalized in the production of manuscripts.

Ancient writing in Greek and Latin followed a common procedure of transcription whereby a scribe composes (often in a strong sense) a text at the direction and dictation of the author. With the use of the requisite language alphabet and the associations of sounds and lettering, the scribe transcribes and composes by means of common practice and codes of exchange for sound and graphic markings to present word signs on the page.

Such manuscripts were devoid of punctuation. Authors did not dictate punctuation markings, and scribes did not provide punctuation to their transcriptions.[2] Readers introduced the marks of punctuation into Christian scriptures just as all such marks were added by readers into other classical and Hellenistic manuscripts. Later copyist and editors might copy these marks introduced by another reader in their reproduction of the work. Or as readers of the text, after marking the script themselves in keeping with their reading, scribes might copy or have another copy their appointed manuscript. Thus, the predominant features of ancient manuscripts were that a text was composed in a continuous script of capital lettering without spacing to separate words from one another and without punctuation. As M. B. Parkes expressed it, ancient writings were composed in "neutral continuous scripts." Such "neutrality" on Parkes's terms concerns the lack of later techniques of punctuation, the creation of lower case letters which lead to the differential use of upper and lower-case letters, and stylized spacing which would serve "to resolve structural uncertainties in a text, and to signal nuances of semantic significance" (Parkes 1992, 1). The incorporation of such techniques into an ancient manuscript served to score the neutral continuous scripts by a reader who sought to establish sentential order by making evident the cohesive articulations which the reader discerned in reading the script. Such order came by way of the differentiation of one sentence from the others by parsing the lexically undifferentiated ambiguous script. Sentential order performed by the use of marks of distinction (or otherwise called punctuation) served as a refinement of the continuous phrasing. Further, the use of punctuation served to make evident at least for the reader scoring one's own copy of a work as expressive of a cohesive articulation of the script as determined by the reader. That is the

---

2   One notable exception was Cicero who would return to the penultimate copy of the polished transcript and appoint the script as he preferred it to be read prior to the work being copied and released.

continuous script was neutral to the extent that a reader would differentiate one word from another, and one sentence from another in the script on his or her own terms, and grammatical and literary judgment.

The inventive processes of fashioning non-alphabetical graphic marks and defining their function in service to the discernment and articulation of sentential order in the "neutral continuous scripts" of Christian scriptures evolved over millennium. The introduction of the rudimentary mark of punctuation was commonly little more than the addition of a point or period to the script.[3] The purpose of such pointing a script at the discretion of the reader instituted at the most elementary level that the reader indicated a *pause* in reading for *effect* (Parkes 1992). But while the mark to pause may be at least clear to another reading the previously punctuated script of an earlier reader, the effect of the pause as determined by the reader who supplied the mark, is far less clear. That the reader who supplied the mark discerned that the script as read suggested some effect at a specific point where the period mark was inserted is clear. For it is assumed that every application of a period or point conveyed some decision or preference of a reader as to both the site and the effect. Thus, it follows that for each appointing of the script there is a pause and an effect. However, given the lack of codes and conventions, and the minimal repertory of graphic non-alphabetical marks of punctuation, at best one might speculate as to the effect the period signified. That the reader found the text as meriting the introduction of the period in the script was an action that is open for review and assessment by subsequent readers. Thus, the effect of the appointed script for a reader, the effect of the pause in the appointed reading, was at the discretion of the reader who supplied the mark. But the reader who introduced the point/period into the script might have been the only person to know what the effective purpose of such a marking served. All punctuation of Christian scriptures was added by readers who exercised a reader's choice for appointing the "neutral" script of a text to indicate the point at which to pause in the reading to occasion an effect. And once a script was appointed by a reader, it did not follow that a subsequent reader was obligated to accept the previous reader's sense of the text, or the decision to punctuate the text at a specific site or for a particular effect.

Scribes and copyists, as well as the readers of the manuscripts, did not have at their disposal in antiquity nor as late as the concluding centuries of the first millennium comprehensive operational systems of punctuation to appoint

---

3   What is taken as a "period" in print medium referred in the manuscript traditions as a "point" or "pointing". Likewise, what is now referred to in print as a point was in ancient and medieval manuscripts referenced as a period (Brown 1999).

their writing, copying or reading which were universally shared even within the confines of a specific language or dialect. For aside from limited attempts at the systemization of such marking of a script, the sense of the demarcated pause was more often than not ambiguous and open to interpretation by readers of a text that had been appointed by another.

The developed systems deployed space to style (1) the separation of words one from another, (2) to mark paragraph breaks, (3) to mark the end of a sentence, and (4) to indication by means of indentation or by hanging the first word out past the left margin of the text or column to indicate the beginning of a new paragraph. These uses of stylized spacing added by scribes in the reproduction of the continuous script in later hand produced copies of Christian scripture also began to incorporate the use of punctuation in a desire to discern if not express the sense of the text as read by someone, and to exercise authority on the establishment of the sentential order of the text.

In what follows, the semiotic mechanisms of quoting of or from scripture, and quotations found or assessed to be integrated in scripture, and the semiotic procedures for punctuating the ancient scripts serve to effect two major developments concerning scripture in the evolving of Christian societies and cultures. I argue that the mechanism whereby the source script is harvested for pericopes that are then incorporated as quotations in Christian discourse serve in a strong sense in the "rewriting" of Christian scriptures. The effect of such "rewriting" serves to correlate Christian scriptures as harvested quotations with a convictional discourse. Thus "rewriting" the scriptures by means of the discursive incorporation of quotations drawn from holy writ serves to reframe and so reconfigure the sense of the phrase harvested as to authorize and advance one's own position in competition if not contests with other emergent sectarian Christian associations.

The semiotic mechanisms of punctuation served "to score" the neutral continuous script such that the addition inscribed back into the script a reading of the scriptures such that the scored text produced the reader's rendition of the work in subsequent reading performance. In addition, given the association of a specific reading performance of the text, the rendition could serve to support and advance one's own specific Christian discursive venture. I address this operation when considering Augustine consideration of such demarcation in his work *On Christian Teaching*.

From the earliest drawing of quotations from the scriptures by readers and the earliest markings added by readers to the source script with the rudimentary appointing of the continuous neutral script, the production of Christian discourse has deployed two interrelated and interdependent semiotic mechanisms. Moreover, these semiotic techniques of quoting the source text for discursive purposes and of scoring the source pages of the text with punctuation to support the harvesting of useful quotations and the reading performance of the source text in support of discursive purposes persist and are pervasive in all manner of Christian life, culture and society.

Modern readers accustomed to modern machine manufactured print material often find it difficult to consider let alone comprehend that much if not most of our operating procedures for writing, printing and reading are rather late mostly modern inventions. Christian scriptures were produced as were all ancient Greek manuscripts including the classical works of ancient philosophy and literature, under very different procedural systems of writing and reading from what evolved over the millennium.

Elementary Reading of Continuous Script

In educational institutions in the west one of the first tasks is the teaching and learning to read and write. And in learning to read and write one of our elementary concerns is with how to read and write words. Early on we know how to identify a word on a page. It comprises a set of letters which are set off from other words with the use of space. When I learned to read English in first grade, I read a book (as best as I can remember) that looked something like the text below which the class was instructed to read out loud together to our teacher Mrs. Peterson.

> See. See Dick. See Dick and Jane. See Dick run. See Jan run. See Dick run up the hill. See Jane run up the hill. See Dick and Jane run up the hill. See Spot run.

If we were learning to read Greek as students at the beginning of the Common Era, our experience with the text would be quite different. Taking aside that students were reading a Greek language text, the text they would have read would differ in that they would be instructed on how to read a hand-written script which resembled the following:

SEEDICKSEEDICKANDJANESEEDICKRUNSEEJANERUNSEEDICK
RUNUPTHEHILLSEEJANERUNUPTHEHILLSEEDICKANDJANERUNUP
THEHILLTOGETHERSEESPOTRUN

Please excuse my use of the English language in this illustration. Such a language did not exist then, but I use English to make my point to English speaking readers. Further the grammar of Greek (whether ancient or modern) differs significantly from modern English. My point is to exhibit the features of the neutral scripts which would be found in an ancient manuscript which students were expected to learn to read.

And the most obvious features we have covered are all capital letters in a continuous line without punctuation and spacing between words. Given these features, the skills needed for reading included that students learn to differentiate words from one another and to comprehend the grammatical association of words.

Parkes notes, "the merit of *scriptio continua* was that it presented the reader with a *neutral* text. To introduce graded pauses while reading involved an interpretation of the text, an activity requiring literary judgment and therefore one properly reserved to the reader" (Parkes 1992, 11). The literary judgment required of someone learning to read Greek in antiquity began with the parsing of the script into words. Reading and interpretation of the continuous neutral text were intimately associated. Reading is of course an active intellectual practice. But ancient Greek language manuscripts presented the reader with a significant intellectual technical challenge of determining the weave of the script and the sense of the writing as the reader was expected to figure out how to parse one word from another and determine their associations. It was not so much that the reader was expected to un-weave the script, as forced to decide upon reading and considering the wording, how to perform the textual cohesive script as woven language (*textus*).

Returning to our first grade-reading example, parsing the words is just the beginning. At which points should the reader pause so as to functionally construct the script into phrase units or sentences? Such "judgment" is to "sentence" the script. Our example is rather simple. But the options for parsing the last couple of words present an ambiguity which determines different interpretations of the entire short piece.

SEEDICKANDJANERUNUPTHEHILLTOGETHERSEESPOTRUN

See Dick and Jane run up the hill together. See Spot run.

Or is it,

See Dick and Jane run up the hill together. "See Spot." "Run."

Imagine that Spot is not the fun loving playful puppy imagined in the first grade reader, but is more akin to the mad dog Tim Johnson, shot by Atticus in "To Kill a Mockingbird". See Spot run could be parsed such that "See Spot" and

"Run" are now a set of discreet commands conjoined by sequence, and by a presumption that if you see Spot you will understand that the consequence is to run away and escape the mad dog. The denotative significance of the command "See Spot run" could thus suggest "See Spot running" or so parsed that the sequence of commands is "see Spot" as in to look at Spot (who is not being described as running), followed by a command to Dick and Jane: "RUN" (Spot is a rabid dog). By first grade most pupils in my class could tell you a story or two about a mad dog. Such was life in rural south Alabama.

The privilege and responsibility of the reader to demarcate the sentential order of a Greek manuscript provided a means by which a reader could exercise a prerogative such that the reader's identification of a quotation in a script and the reader's harvested phrase as a quotation might be taken into account by their use of the period to mark and so parse the script. The reader's choice on how to punctuate the continuous script could serve as the means for indicating for the reader how to articulate the script when reading in keeping with the reader's interpretation of the text.

My use of quotation marks in parsing the three last words in our example concerning Dick, Jane and Spot as two distinctive commands would have been impossible in antiquity. In fact, the history and development of the repertory of punctuation marks is in many ways a product of late medieval and modern western intellectual history given the prominence of punctuation in all venues of the material culture of reading and writing in modern western civilization. Quotation punctuation marks were invented as typeface and introduced in print in the 16th century by Aldus Manutius (the younger), a Venetian editor and printer. Manutius published his own work *Orthographiae ratio* ("System of Orthography") in 1566 in which he stated plainly that the purpose for the invention and use of marks of punctuation were to provide syntactical clarity, rather than as indications for the elocution or performance of the script in a public reading (Brown 2007). Of course, the efficacy of marking a phrase as a quotation with the introduction of the open quote and close quote typeface to demarcate the quote provided syntactical clarity as well as provided an efficient alternative to printers who previously would set the type of a quoted phrase in a different font.

As concerns the Gospels, the words of Jesus eventually came to be more clearly set out in type by means of the addition of quotation marks to designate quoted phrases of the Lord as publishers identified them. Such quotations within the script so punctuated or by means of a different type face or as in early twentieth century productions of the King James Bible which produced the quotations of Jesus in red inked lettering in contrast to the black inked letter of the majority of the text, served to propagate a discursive venture within many ecclesial institutions and societies. For the quotations, so punctuated or inked came to play the role of the sign, as signifying phrases which came to be venerated as the precise words of the Lord. For it was as if the red-letter wording attributed to Jesus signified the words as if they had been spoken by Jesus, *as if* they were in some sense a direct recording of what Jesus said transcribed in the script of the Gospel literature.

Early attempts among medieval copyist and scribes who sought to systematize the demarcations of the use of the period to convey some sense of pause and articulation in the script appear to have limited success both in terms of the persistence of such codifications and as regards the reach of such codes and signs beyond provinces. The explicit marking of the continuous script of a Greek manuscript into discrete units was at the discretion of a reader in keeping with the social practices and the material culture of writing then in place in the Greco-Roman world. For it remained the reader who could choose to insert or not to insert a period as a means for reminding the reader where and when to pause in order to articulate the termination of the phrase when performing a text in a public reading.

Parkes argues that while there were limits to the number of ways in which the linguistic structure may be interpreted; nevertheless, an examination of the punctuation in surviving copies of the same text reveals a surprising amount of variety (Parkes 1991, 265–66). And it is his point that we return to consider at several points in the pages to follow.[4]

Parkes notes in his minimalist pragmatic assessment of the continuous script that the addition of the "period," the most commonly used graphic mark added by readers to punctuate the continuous script, served in most instances with little code or convention except to convey for the reader who added the mark that it would be useful to "pause" reading at this point of the script for "effect." But the effect of the pause is so individual or if shared so local that the

---

4 Jerome's *Vulgate* translation of the Greek script employed codes of articulation not evident or at least not common in Greek manuscripts to explicitly indicate his decision as to how the text was to be divided into discrete units. Jerome began each new sentence as he discerned or made a judgment with the first word of a new sentence extended hanging out over the left margin usually by the width of the first letter. The identification of the limit of the discreet sentential unit would then conclude what was to be written on a line, and which was marked as having terminated with a period. This exaggerated use of style—the hanging first line of the sentence and the concluding of a sentence on a line with a period serves to illustrate the operation as performed by Jerome to demarcate the sentential unit of the text.

purpose of the "appointing" maybe lost. That the reading is to pause is clear. But the purpose of the pause, the effect to be orchestrated by pausing, may be lost even upon the reader who provided the mark if upon returning to the appointed copy the reader wonders: "Why did I add this point here? What did I mean by it?" The reader upon review of the script may recall the reading rendition so marked, or may have to discern the reading anew, or even abandon the reading so marked. The use of the appointment supplied no information given that there was no operational code for what to make of the period other than the pause it signaled for the reader.

Without a convention to establish agreed upon operational codes as to the meaning of different graphic signs, the mark added to the continuous script served to signify that "some" sense as regards how to read the text is noted, but provided no information in the script as to the specifics of what the sign meant or how to articulate the verse besides or except to pause.

That the appointment of the continuous script with a period "signaled" a pause is to acknowledge that the use of punctuation served as a sign, with at least a minimalist codification that the reader was to take a pause in reading. Thus, at a rudimentary level, at an early point in the history of reading and marking punctuation in ancient continuous Greek manuscripts of the New Testament, the point was an elementary sign which functioned to present a pause in reading. And in this instance, the appointment in the continuous script may on Peircean terms be an indexical indicator. For the period was the only non-alphabetical marking in the continuous script which could not be "read" as a word or a sound, and yet represented something other and more to be understood in the process of reading. At minimum, the period indexed a pause. Otherwise, the period could also have indicated at least for the reader who applied the period that some other function was to occur in conjunction with the pause. And that sense of the period as pause, and pause as something more had to do with its pragmatic application given that in most instances the placement of a mark of punctuation was not supported by code and convention for how to read a mark of punctuation in text.

It might have been clear to someone who listened to the reader who so marked the pause what the punctuation provided in the reading performance, but then the context for making sense of the use of the punctuation mark would have to do with experiencing the reader's elocution of the grammatical sense of the script as performed. Otherwise, the meaning of the use of punctuation for a pause is open for discussion and decision. Without the conventions of code or the pragmatic contextualization of the reading event and the operational function of the reader's so marking the script the sense of the entry of the mark into the continuous script was idiosyncratic as too the sense of the pause aside from the pause in reading.[5]

In time, as I shall argue in our discussion of Augustine, the emergent use of the demarcation of the script served to establish the fitting out of the script into a sentential order in which each sentence was marked as a complete thought. This was in some strong sense for Augustine the purpose for the appointing of the text of scripture with periods. And as I argue, the purpose for appointing the sentences was motivated in part by Augustine's desire that the script be fitted out with punctuation such that it provided an order which protected the integrity and availability of his preferred quotations (Greek περικοπαι, Latin *sententiae*) which supported orthodox convictions, and served to stymie heretical sentential orders in service to their preferred harvesting of quotations.

Sentences and Quotations

To state what is obvious for a modern writer and reader, a sentence is commonly defined as a basic grammatical unit that is expected to be clearly demarcated by the use of punctuation such that the end of the sentence is marked with a period, a question mark or an exclamation mark. The mark concluding the sentence is followed by a space before the beginning of the next sentence is indicated with the use of an upper-case letter to set off the first word of a script predominately written or printed in lower case letters. The deployment of spacing serves to separate words from one another and each sentence is further distinguished from the sentence before and after by additional space. This display of sentential punctuation and spacing styles all serve to encode the work with information on how to identify and read this basic unit of writing for a modern reader of published texts. The demarcation of the complete sentence with the period, question or exclamation mark, and the internal sentential structures evident in the use of commas, colons and semi-colons, with the use of quotations marks to include a quotation, in concert with styles of spacing fore and aft, and the rules of capitalization differentiate the first term

---

5 Another reader might find the placement of the mark helpful for understanding that by pausing in reading the script, the earlier reader is suggesting something about the script. But without some shared context or shared system of codes for reading the script, neither the mark nor the pause conveys the sense of the added mark. The intent of the addition may be unfathomable or irretrievable. All that is clear is that the placement of the mark in the continuous script suggested that the reader who chose to mark the script conveyed to those who followed that some sense for pausing was made without conveying information by means of a shared code as to what sense is articulated concerning the pause in reading the script, or how the pause articulated the sense of the content. Without code the sign of the punctuation is senseless. For without code, the "mark" is no sign.

of a new sentence. Once function of punctuation, specifically commas, semi-colons and periods, are employed to indicate the differentiation of the groupings of words as units and in some cases the relationship between these units, "Omissions or misused marks may force a reader to go over a passage two or three times to get its intended meaning ..." (Perrin, Smith and Corder 1968, 16). But the issue when reading an ancient manuscript is that given that there was no punctuation provided by author or scribe, the lack of punctuation was neither misuse nor omission. Because the very project of transcription/composition did not possess the graphic non-alphabetical infrastructure of codes and conventions for such markings in the punctuating of the articulations of a page.

The harvesting of quotations from Christian scripture, and the introduction of marks of punctuation into a script for the purpose of distinguishing sentential structure and order were choices made at the discretion of an ancient reader. Other readers may concur as to the significance and purpose of a quote by borrowing the same quote from the source work or by simply repeating the harvested quote as it was employed in the discourse of another without having reviewed the source work from which it was quoted, cut or extracted.

The successful harvesting of quotations that are repeated and performed by others establishes a legacy whereby the script or text has been "scored" to the extent to which the now popular quotation comes to present if not represent the author and work quoted. The power of a quotation in a discursive legacy is how the quotation conveys its deployed content in the discourse with the authority and power of the source author and work.

The successful punctuation of the script into a sentential order that serves a common reading of the work may become in time how the work is copied such that the earlier continuous and unpunctuated script is functionally replaced and forgotten as the conventional reading is instituted in the source by means of punctuation and habit. Thus, under the persuasion of the constructed sentential order integrated into the discursive legacy, the sentential order acquires or shares the legitimacy bestowed upon the work and its author. But the conventional status of the continuous script fades.

What is lost with these developments as quotes are deployed without regard for how they were selected and constructed in shared discursive legacies, and as the old continuous script is scored into a sentential order in accordance with choices made under the influence of a dominating discursive legacy, is the evidence that such ventures present choices which were made at the discretion of readers who choose what to quote and preferences for how to read a script. Thus, under the influence of such preferences that come to dominate shared discursive legacies of quoting and reading, the possibility of individual and alternative preferences on how to read and quote a work can be lost. Or simply, such differences are just not evident or available. Reading and quoting became learned, rehearsed and enforced often through repetition. And under such rote practice the discretion of the classical reader may all but vanish under the weight of custom and production.

It is important to understand that to read aloud an ancient Greek script or Latin script which is in its "neutral" state as a continuous script without punctuation required the eloquent reader to spend time with the manuscript to disentangle the continuous script so as to distinguish individual units of words, phrases, and sentences. Such provided the reader an opportunity to emphasize valued quotations in an endeavor to comprehend how the work is cohesive, how the various parts connect and influence in their articulation of the sense of the work as discerned by the reader.

Parkes notes that there is little evidence prior to the sixth century as to an author's phrasing by means of punctuation to guide a reader. Parkes elaborates his point by noting that there are no manuscripts that have survived from Antiquity which were composed by the hand of their author. And the reason for the absence of autograph material is in part due to the broad practice of authors dictating "one's own works, letters, and even one's own notes, to amanuenses" (Parkes 1992, 9). Thus, if an author supplied punctuation to their own written work they would do so as a reader or editor of a work written out by another. "Because the work of scribes or amanuenses was 'mechanical', they confined themselves to reproducing as faithfully as possible what had been transmitted to them without further interpretation; hence they did not supply punctuation to a text" (Parkes 1992, 9). Their focus as scribes was to render with the alphabet in compliance with the conventions of correlating marks that "meant" the sound in sequence as spoken.

Textual Cohesiveness and Semiotics Textus

Text semiotics analyzes how a text writ large is greater than the sum of its constitutive parts (words, sentences, paragraphs). Roland Barthes reminds us that the modern term "text" which comes from the Latin *textus* is derived from the past participle (*text-*) of the verb *texere* meaning "to weave, to plait, to fit together" (Barthes 1979, 76). The challenge is to account for how the text is a cohesive, articulating and coherent *textus*, a Latin term introduced by Quintilian that presents written language as material language *woven* in the production of a tissue/*textus* by the art and techniques of transcription. A text so conceived is "that which is woven or fitted together; a texture, structure: context." Barthes developed his use of *textus* towards the notion of intertextuality by which he argued that all texts have other texts woven in them to some degree. I made much of this in my earlier work where I was concerned to account for the presence of quoted material woven into the biblical *textus* of Paul's letters. My concern in this study is to consider the issues that arise when material quoted from a biblical text for discursive purposes draws upon phrases that have been incorporated in the biblical text as quotation. In short, the issues arise when one quotes a phrase which is itself a quotation. How does the presence, articulation, cohesiveness and coherence of quoted material as incorporated in a scriptural text complicate the production of quoting the text for discursive purposes?

In his discussion of the differences between semiotics and semantics, Paul Ricoeur contends that

> The object of semiotics—the sign—is merely virtual. Only the sentence is actualized as the event of speaking. This is why there is no way of passing from the word as a lexical sign to the sentence by mere extension of the same methodology to a more complex entity. The sentence is not a larger or more complex word, it is a new entity. It may be decomposed into words, but the words are something other than short sentences. A sentence is a whole irreducible to the sum of its parts. It is made up of words, but it is not a derivative function of its words. A sentence is made up of signs, but is not itself a sign.
> RICOEUR 1976, 7

I would argue that while there is no way of passing from the word as a lexical sign to the sentence by mere extension of the same methodology in which the sentence is not simply a larger or more complex "word," the more complex entity of a discourse is no mere sentence. A discourse is a more complex entity which is more than and other than a sentence. Or, a discourse is not an indifferent collection of autonomous sentences which do not articulate cohesively. These organic like constructions do not commit the generic fallacy that each subsequent entity is an extension of the structures of the previous. Deconstruction does not explain away the emergent composition because the constitutive parts are not in sum the whole. Construction exceeds the constitutive parts. To deconstruct the *textus* is to discern how a composition is woven or textured language. To simply untwist and pull the weave apart is not to deconstruct the *textus*. Such taking apart of a construction is better characterized as demolition, the taking apart of a construction such that the constructing, the weave and texture are destroyed.

Ricoeur continues,

> There is therefore no linear progression from the phoneme to the lexeme and then on to the sentence and to linguistic wholes larger than the sentence. Each stage requires new structures and a new description. The relation between the two kinds of entities may be expressed in the following way, following the French Sanskritist Emile Benveniste: language relies on the possibility of two kinds of operations, integration into larger wholes, and dissociation into constitutive parts. The sense proceeds from the first operation, the form from the second.
>
> RICOEUR 1976, 7

I argue that there is no way of passing from a sentence or phrase by mere extension of the same methodology to a more complex entity like an argument, story or letter. In the instance of a letter that replies to oral and written messages, the complex letter's *textus* is not simply a larger collection of the constitutive sentences. The totality of sentences in a text do not constitute the text. Rather, the sense, the meaning effect of a text is not the simple accumulation of the sentences. A text is not a derivative of its sentences. Rather the letter is woven so as to provide a texture, a structure which exceeds the structures of the autonomous sentences which are woven together. The quotes incorporated in a letter which replies need not be composed as a chain of positive conjunctions. For the structure of a letter which quotes and replies becomes evident in the play between parts, in the tensions which express complex positioning or maybe engage in an outright argument.

The move to the dissolution into constitutive parts reveals how a *textus* "composes" or "constructs" a meaningful discourse out of different units or units that are different. The composing exceeds the sense of any isolated unit incorporated into the text as the *textus* of a work, the sense of a *textus* is occasioned by the articulations that provide for the cohesiveness of the constitutive parts into a larger context.

Thus, just as a word serves as a sign within the sentence which provides context, a sentence serves as a sign in the context of a theme or thesis. A sentential unit incorporated as a "total" or "totality" into the emergent composition that incorporates and integrates the constitutive sentences and provides by means of context the status and sense of the constitutive parts in the cohesive articulating texture of woven language.

If we are to synchronize our structures of interpretation to the structures of the source text, might that simply mean that we need to imitate or at least acknowledge the structures of the source text in our consideration. But to do this, to imitate the structures of the text we find ourselves addressing the limitations of our association with the "text" as it has evolved over the centuries. For the evolution of the structures rely upon the interactions of syntax and semantics which are predominantly functions of sentential grammatical order, which are styled by the use of punctuation in the determination of the status of the sentence units and their relation to one another. The contributions of spacing and punctuation for composing and reading a text cannot be over stated.

But what would we go on if we are attempting to comprehend the structures of the continuous scripts of say Paul's epistle to the Corinthians? Spacing and punctuation are foreign inventions that intervene in the affairs of reading and comprehending these ancient Greek scripts. And even if we are able to approximate a lexical exchange of modern English words for Greek words of the texts of 1 Corinthians, and we are confident or at least comfortable with the rendering of the Greek sentences with modern English sentences, how would we proceed to synchronize the structures? What evidence would we draw upon from the ancient continuous script?

And so we come to a problem as regards the hypothesis by Parkes that the manuscripts of antiquity, and the earliest manuscripts of the works eventually incorporated into the New Testament, were "neutral" scripts—composed in continuous scripts with capital Greek letters without spacing or marks of punctuation.

Punctuation as Technique and Technology for Contextualizing a Script

The evident use of marks of punctuation often emergent, inchoate and idiosyncratic in Ancient, Hellenistic and early medieval manuscripts, in time evolved with writing, reading and copying. Following many attempts and failures to establish broad-based consensus concerning the punctuation of manuscripts, conventions and codes of punctuation eventually resulted in enriched semiotic operational systems with the invention and advanced development of the techniques and technologies of machine printing and eventually machine composing. Thus, the systems of style and punctuation flourished as broad-based codes for writing and reading only with the technological advantages which facilitated the remastering of the works in print. Under the conventions and procedural codes of publishing houses which sought to operationalize and standardize grammar and style at least as instituted practices in their manufacturing of printed works, punctuation marks both flourished and attained broad-based consensus as to their design, use and purpose. Thus, text design served to manifest a desired effective reading

Of special concern as regards the remastering of ancient Greek manuscripts of Christian scripture in modern machine production is the question as to the semiotic status which marks of punctuation play in the production of printed rescored Greek language texts. Punctuation marks serve as expressive of the codification of the signs (words, phrases and sentences) of a text as in what sense a reader makes of the associated words in phrases and sentences as established by the editor or publisher of a printed text. Further, punctuation marks may also come to serve as "signs" under the procedural systems of publishing influenced by the "conventions" of reading and writing. Modern publishing of ancient works thus came to restyle ancient discourses under the influence of modern conventions which were operationalized by enriched practices of print text formation in which punctuation was added to the ancient language scripts in modern print production. Added marks of punctuation and introduced stylized spacing to ancient continuous scripts in modern print production of Greek New Testaments simultaneously serve as a play of code and sign in the "editing" and production of such printing, as well as in the reading of such published writings. Semiotic questions arise as to the status of punctuation markers. Are they employed and deployed in the script as markers of interpretation if not also translation of the Greek script?

In the centuries following the technological advances of print production, the techniques and technologies for punctuating the script with the new methods and marks for designating a quotation introduced in print production of the Greek New Testament resulted in identified quotations by readers being crafted by publishers *as* quotations in print. Such houses sometimes employed different type face or font to indicate those phrases judged to be quotations. The play of quoting an authority, and the demands for representing one's sources became an honest means of presenting the debt any writer owed ancient authors and texts, and which modern religious writers owed scriptural authors and texts.

Regarding the letters of Paul, it is often assumed that what was written in the epistles were what Paul instructed his secretary to transcribe. The crafting of quotations as occurring in the letters of Paul contained no punctuation marks to signal that a phrase was a quotation. Because the assumption was that what was written, except in those occasional phrases which were widely judged to be obvious plain examples of quotations included in the text by Paul and entered by his secretary, were authored by Paul. Meaning, the epistles in totality were in some strong sense a quotation of what Paul "dictated" to his secretary in the production of the transcripts. Even when Paul quotes another in his epistles, the apparent plainer "quoted" phrases were taken to be recycled by Paul from a source (written or orally delivered), and in a rather straightforward sense (though not without complications) therefore composed or recomposed by Paul as he dictated his letter. That is Paul's content was and is assumed by the authority of the dominant movements of Christianity to be a coherent discourse by the Apostle in which the quoted matter articulated *support* of Paul's own position.

The crafted pericope drawn from the letters by readers served as a sign, signifying as a quote something other and more than just the content of the phrase that was drawn out for quoting the epistles. For the sense of a quote drawn from Paul's letters stood for his authority as the Apostle to the Gentiles. Such drawn pericopes incorporated into the discursive life of Christian society and culture as venerated holy writ, served as signifiers for the "whole" of Paul and all his letters, if not in some crude sense, Christian scripture. Thus, it would be normal to hear or read some declare "Paul wrote that 'the greatest of these is love'" or "The Bible says that 'the greatest of these is love'." Or, "The apostle stated that 'it is good for a man not to touch a woman'." This sense of a quote as serving to encapsulate the author and the work, if not the biblical corpus, as a totality, will be a topic of discussion later in this study. For now, it is sufficient to note that a quote often serves as a token for a totality or a token for some inchoate image of a totality.

What follows the critical analysis of the discourse associated with the harvesting of quotations from Christian scripture is to consider the concreteness of the text, to inquire into the *textus* of the work venerated as scripture, which is quite concretely on Parkes's term a "neutral script." At issue in the reading of an ancient Greek manuscript is how are we to make sense of the neutral continuous script absent the operational systems and signs modern readers are accustomed and trained to decipher as we read. The repertoire of graphic non-alphabetical marks embedded in the scripts we write, the texts we type, and all that we read both handwritten and typed are persistent and pervasive. Our operational customs of spacing to separate words and paragraphs make determining such elementary differentiations a labor when working with manuscripts. Such markings are such a natural part of our commerce in the world that such notes occur and influence our reading often without our taking notice until we come upon a difficult phrase whose status and articulation are difficult to comprehend and read due to a lack, or excess or problematic use of punctuation and space.

Lacking such obvious techniques and conventions of writing and reading which communicate the distinctions and articulations between phrases, distinguishing sentences and paragraphs in an ancient Greek manuscript, the modern reader is left with discerning the relations of words in the script by making determinations as to how the rich structures of Greek grammar evident how Greek words convey their syntactical qualities in the use of word endings. The sentential or lexical division of the continuous script is ambiguous in most instances. But the relations of words are often characterized being articulated as cohesive phrases by means of the interactions given of morphological endings and articles. Sentential structures are more than the syntax and semantics of Greek phrasing. That is, the reader both past and present, when considering the syntax and the semantics of an ancient Greek language script is left with the responsibility of what "sentence" to compose given the latitude provided by the grammatical possibilities. Such texts are commonly far more "open" (Eco 1979) to the discretion of a reader as to how the text is composed than readers of modern publications that draw upon the repertory of punctuation and style options in composition and production. Modern readers are accustomed to such judgments made by the publisher and author.

The openness in Greek manuscripts of works incorporated in the New Testament is of course foreclosed in "modernized" publications of the Greek New Testament. Those who only work from such scored and remastered productions of the Greek New Testament may fail to discern that what they are reading, what is being studied is concretely different if not foreign from the earliest available sources. The division of labor with publishers supplying a remastered Greek New Testament provides a short-cut for those teaching and learning how to read and translate the Greek texts. With words spaced out, sentential order determined and punctuated such that the decisions concerning sentence type and structure is conveyed with periods, commas, colons, question and exclamation marks, as well as appointed with quotation marks, such that the student and teacher can concentrate on the pedagogical task of learning the systems of Greek grammar and vocabulary in training for basic translation.

To consider again the ancient manuscripts as different is to think of them as foreign in the strongest sense of the term. From the Latin *foris*, meaning "outside" influenced the English *fore* as in "before". A sense of the root is played in such terms as forest, forfeit, and foreclose. An early use of foreign as in "a chamber foreign" referred to an outside privy. In the 15th century "foreigner" came to replace "stranger" as someone from another country, someone from outside one's own, or someone not belonging. The sense of alien from *alienus* (Latin) as in belonging to other persons or things not one's own came to be strongly associated with the sense of foreign, including the introduction in medical terminology of a foreign object or substance as embedded in tissues of one's own body.

Beginning with a domesticated scripture prepared to serve a specific sectarian discourse, presented the script already scored to instate specific social desires and cultural dreams, served to vouch safe the ecclesial institutions as if what was quoted and discussed were a total piece. Such coherence served

THE SENSE OF QUOTING 35

to establish the social and political systems and structures for an economy of advantage and disadvantage. But the concreteness of the continuous script behind and before these productions, scoring, manufacturing and operational processes is all but lost in those who belong to the effective institutions.

The texts available are so thoroughly re-engineered and edited that contemporary readers might be unaware of all the production, all the additions, and all the editing by so many hands over the ages. A return to the available manuscripts entails that we critically examine by comparison all the ways that the texts have been refashioned. When teaching or making a public presentation as a lecturer, I find it useful to reverse the mastering of the text in a manner that is similar to the techniques for reverse engineering an ancient artifact by archeologist. My colleagues who engage in such endeavors seek to work backwards to discover what tools might have been employed in the production, and as well to imagine how the tools might have been conceived and produced. And then they proceed to discern how the artifact might have been constructed using such ancient tools.

Not only are the means of producing ancient manuscripts foreign in relation to modern writing and publishing, but the ancient reader's discretion in punctuating the ancient manuscripts—albeit by modern standards rudimentary and idiosyncratic—is foreign to us all. Working only from modern productions of the text whether a Greek New Testaments or the New Testament in translation, what we read has been so manufactured and remanufactured that we proceed as if we are in the blind as to what all has been produced for us. What discretions rested with the individual ancient reader performing the text in their communities have been usurped more recently by modern institutions of churches and publishers alike who have rendered the text suitable for consumption. But the process began so long ago, that to cry foul as if the manipulation were something recently committed, or only recently committed is to miss the point.

I seek to reverse the processes in part because I think it is useful for the class or audience or reader to experience some aspects of the concrete manuscripts at a point prior to the onset of the remastering of the manuscripts by publishers and the conventions of rescoring of the scripture. I illustrate the concreteness of a continuous script which is free of spacing and punctuation so as to draw into play the sense of the script by engaging in a process of de-scoring, and de-mastering of the effective scored and mastered script. The available artifacts of concrete ancient texts of Christian scriptures are the manuscripts that are valued and venerated as the source or best available sources of the works. The pages of scripture available for reading, study and devotion are the work of multiple ventures of editing, production and translation that began with the act of transcription as the author dictated the work often in conversation with the scribe.

I project for viewing images of pages and close up segments from ancient biblical manuscripts in order to prepare and provide a context for the exercise. Given my interest in the letters of Paul, I commonly share images of full pages as well as cropped close up images of segments of the manuscripts of Codex Sinaiticus, Codex Vaticanus, and Codex Chester Beatty. In conjunction with the images I play upon the conception of translation and interpretation as conversational as proposed by Paul Ricoeur (Ricoeur 2004). Or, more precisely conversational reading. Clearly almost all my students and usually all of the audience in public lectures have no acquaintance with the Greek language, let alone ancient manuscripts. So, I take one of the standard, academically credible translations of a biblical text and I copy the text on a handout. But rather than simply transferring the modern text or cut and paste the text to the handout, I "de-score" the English translation such that the English text is brought to simulate the continuous script. Thus, de-scored and de-mastered in accordance with the lack of special structures and punctuation in keeping with the ancient Greek manuscript, the English translation provides a heuristic device which serves as a useful pedagogical technique for providing some limited insight into just how foreign are some of the features of the old manuscript.

IAPPEALTOYOUBRETHRENBYTHENAMEOFOURLORDJESUSCHRIST
THATALLOFYOUAGREEANDTHATTHEREBENODISSENSIONSAMONG
YOUBUTTHATYOUBEUNITEDINTHESAMEMINDANDTHESAMEJUDGE
MENTWHATIMEANISTHATEACHONEOFYOUSAYSIBELONGTOPAULI
TOAPOLLOSITOCEPHASITOCHRISTHASCHRISTALLOCATEDHIMSELF

The result is that the English text is now presented without the added techniques of spacing, lower case lettering and punctuation so as to present the modern translation without the expected characteristics features in accord with the styles and codes of an ancient Greek manuscript—only my examples are not handwritten. Which is good given the poor quality of my penmanship. Further, there are no paragraph indicators to structure the script on the page. The obvious limits of this heuristic device concern the significant differences between ancient Greek and English grammatical presentation and the differences concerning the importance of word order in English related to the cohesiveness of the text. The status of a Greek term is effected by the term's ending which conveys the part of speech which each term plays in the local vicinity of the script. However, the determination of the beginning and ending of a sentence are assessed by the reader based on the interplay of syntax, semantics and pragmatics. And such discretion as to sentential order may lead to significantly different renditions of the script.

Modern readers who find ancient Greek manuscripts difficult to "parse" given the continuous script in all capital letters and bereft of punctuation might assess that somehow such texts are simply "lacking" the necessities of code and convention for making good sense of the wording and the articulations of the text. And they would be correct if and only if such "lacking" bespeaks the sense that the ancient procedural systems were themselves indecipherable for ancient readers or at least thoroughly ambiguous. But to assess that the ancient manuscripts were so "lacking" bespeaks how significantly different the procedural systems we modern readers bring when encountering or engaging the ancient scripts with our own codes and conventions. And so, our fitting out the script above much like an ancient reader might have appointed an ancient manuscript, is informed by our knowledge and skills for operating through our own language despite the "loss" of our accustomed punctuation and spacing as provided by the publishers. The means and the styles of order and structure may be different, but each language under the procedural codes and shared conventions nevertheless support our navigating different texts.

Roman Jakobson "emphasized that the production and interpretation of texts depends upon the existence of codes or conventions for communication" (Jakobson 1990, 15). Thus for Jakobson the code provides "a framework within which signs make sense." In fact, in isolation signs are not meaningful (Jakobson 1990, 15). Chandler goes so far as to argue that "we cannot grant something the status of a sign if it does not function within a code" (Chandler 2002, 147). He goes on to state, "Codes organize signs into meaningful systems which correlate signifiers and signified through structured forms of syntagus and paradigms." Stuart Hall contends that "there is no intelligible discourse without the operation of a code" (Hall 1980, 131). Chandler playing upon the persistent pragmatism of semiotic analysis under the influence of Pierce qualifies that "Codes are not simply "conventions" of communication but rather *procedural systems* of related conventions which operate in certain domains." As such, signs operate in codes which are a procedural system in which signs are able to function in communication (Chandler 2002, 148).

The developments of the codes and signs regarding the framing and fitting out of texts with punctuation was occasioned by problems for which the invention of spacing between words, the use of stylized space to frame out paragraphs and sentences, as well as the invention of punctuation marks to differentiate units and articulations of the continuous script sought to resolve.

All signs occur as signs when they operate in a procedural code of related conventions in certain or specific domains. But to assume that procedural systems for ancient Greek writing and reading were "lacking" what was later invented, is overstated and presumptuous. The procedural systems of ancient writing and reading may have been intellectually challenging and laborious, even for ancient readers. Or at least it may appear to be so, especially for a reader who was burdened by the complex demands for operationalizing the procedures of determining sentential order and articulating the often-nuanced cohesiveness of the script which exhibited an extreme "openness" as to how the script may or was to be read, and what sense was to be made of the script. (I use the sense of "openness" as developed by Eco (1979).) Ancient Greek writing and reading like all other systems of writing and reading, assume semiotic conventions for how signs operate under the influence of shared procedural codes for encoding and decoding the sense of writing and reading. The degree to which such operational codes and conventions were formalized and in which sectors of a society, and the degree to which such functions operated in writing and reading informally are beyond the scope of this study, though clearly of interest to this author.

I have already introduced the problematic feature which particles present to the conception of ancient Greek manuscripts as neutral as such a conception of the continuous script serves to overlook or skip over the particles and fail to acknowledge such lettering in the script as contributing to the reading. The preoccupation with demarcating sentential order and the persistent and long game of the evolution of style and punctuation served to effectively discipline the continuous script. One could lay claim to a neutral text and so cultivate the continuous script, fashioning that which not demarcated by means of scoring, cultivating and mastering the script that it might bear the fruit of quotations for harvest and discursive culture. So cultivated, cultured and harvested, these pericopes could be employed for the manufacturing of cultural artifacts in service to one's own society.

But what if this un-marked continuous script was not so neutral, not so wild, not so un-scored. Then the regime which sought to regiment the resources of the continuous script would be found to be less the means of bringing order than the means of re-ordering, re-scripting, if not remastering a text venerated as scripture in service to one's own purposes which are foreign to the resource, and of a different order than the existing text.

While the momentous creation of the alphabet script for the recording of speech in Greek was transformative for western thought, the use of Greek "particles" also spelled out in the continuous script with the use of the Greek alphabet to present a range of notations concerning the grammatical cohesiveness or logical operations within a script. Such particle notations convey information concerning how the *textus* hangs together. As to whether the particles were also dictated by the author and noted by the scribe, or added by the scribe in transcribing is a matter which I do not address here. It is clear that particles were not added to manuscripts post-production by readers, editors or scribe.

Such particles first begin to be evident in Greek manuscripts during the transition from the fifth to the third centuries before the Common Era. Modern readers might discern that alphabetical notations of particles were employed in ways like the use of later graphic marks which punctuated logical arguments and musical scores as well as the use of graphic punctuation marks to note grammatical articulations in conventional language. But these similarities are not the purpose for my noting the use and status of particles in the script, and certainly should not be taken as an occasion for equating a particular particle with some form of punctuation.

A difference between the inchoate nascent introduction of punctuation into Greek script and the use of particles is that given the dominance of the markers for pause or stopping supplied by the use of the period, the particles which are alphabetical letters imbedded in the continuous script may be better conceived as notations concerning articulations in the performance of reading. But lest we succumb to the later bifurcations of elocution and grammar which was not at work in antiquity, such regard for the reading performance of a text should be understood as both elocution and grammar, such that the grammatical status or grammatical articulation of phrases would be performed as such. In other words, particles contribute to the cohesiveness of a *textus* and present the articulations between phrases or better present phrases as articulating in the continuous flow of the script while the nascent introduction of the period inserted pauses and stops so as to effectively influence the reading and the hearing of the text as read—with effective breathing breaks.

Features and Factors

It is the presumption of critical discourse analysis that language and power are inevitably linked. As Fairclough argues,

> The close analysis of texts in terms of linguistic features like vocabulary, grammar, punctuation, turn-taking, types of speech act and the directness or indirectness of their expression, features of the overall structure of interactions and non-linguistic textual features contribute to our understanding of power relations and ideological processes in discourse.
>
> FAIRCLOUGH 2001, 91

It is generally accepted that what makes discourse analysis critical is not a specific or discrete method. Rather, such analysis concerns how a discourse operates in contests to determine and maintain the distribution of social and political advantages and disadvantages, authority and disfranchisement, domination and subordination, and power and weakness in social and political institutions. The features enumerated by Fairclough serve as factors of the analysis.

Fairclough's list of "features" which are a prominent concern in a discourse analysis of texts are dated. My issue is not with how long-ago Fairclough's analysis of the features under consideration was composed or that such changes are a foot as to render his listed features obsolete. My issue is with the selection of textual features as factors of his analysis that are advanced manufactured products of modern publishing for modern readers. The features enumerated—including the non-linguistic textual features—are themselves instruments of the institutions of modern publishing. Ancient manuscripts of Christian scripture exhibit what Parkes referred to as a "neutral" script—a script free of many of the features on Fairclough's list. Operationalizing Parkes's critical concept concerning the manuscripts as "neutral," brings into sharp relief how the "neutral" scripts came to be fashioned under the persuasion of ancient readers and those who sought in their reading and quoting to draw upon the texts for their own discursive ventures. How readers "punctuated" the script for their own reading, for demarcating or appointing how they read and parsed the text in the early centuries with rudimentary marks were for the most part operationalized idiosyncratically without widely held conventions and codes. The discretionary introduction of non-alphabetical graphic marks of punctuation into the text by the reader to appoint the neutral script served the desires and expressed the ventures of those readers who prepared for and often performed the script in public readings. Often such readers sought to fashion or score the script as they read it in order to better present their reading performance and interpretation of the reading, often to enhance the status of quotable phrases they discovered for their own discursive ventures.

Of special interest is Fairclough's three-dimensional framework in the study of discourse. His three forms of analysis are to be understood as mapping onto one another. These are the (1) analysis of language texts, (2) analysis of discursive practices in the process of text production, distribution and consumption, and finally (3) the analysis of discursive events as socio-cultural practices. I choose to integrate these forms of analysis into the study rather than serving as an organizing schema for which examples are produced. My purpose is to operationalize the integrated and interactive network of analysis such that the formal method fades in bringing forth what is to be discerned in a critical semiotic engagement with the text. Proceeding so is in keeping with critical discourse analysis given that the approach is less preoccupied with policing or managing the production or exhibition of theory and method. The critical move is the exploration of specific structures of discourse, as they are related to sociopolitical structures and struggles that result in inequalities and abuse.

My use of critical discourse analysis concerns the influences on and the consequences of reading and quoting a text that serves in expressing and furthering a social and political agenda. The decisions as to what to emphasize or what is taken to be the information or message of a text serves to institute an economy of advantages and disadvantages. In this vein, the production of quotations from a biblical text for discursive practices serves to further the production, distribution and consumption of the text for social and political purposes. Quoting scripture distributes for consumption phrase bits from the source texts in the production of a discourse which garners authorization by means of quoting. I argue that when such selected quotations from biblical texts are woven into the fabric of a Christian movement's discursive life, the effective distribution of the text by means of quotations in turn serve to exert extraordinary influence back upon the production, distribution and consumption of the biblical text from which the quoted phrase or verse was harvested. Thus, decisions are made which support a specific "scoring" of the neutral biblical manuscript in keeping with the status and function of the quote. Such mastery of the neutral manuscript serves to support the integrity and the legacy of the quoted phrase with and for the effective discursive endeavor. The resulting production, distribution and consumption of subsequent manuscripts incorporate the decisions for punctuating the text and so serve to perpetuate the instituting of the discursive venture in ecclesial social, cultural and political institutions. The production legacy of a manuscript which copies a specific rendition of the script complete with punctuation serves to support a reading of the text which align with a specific set of convictions, beliefs and practices. The advantage sought is that by so producing a rescored manuscript, the biblical text will no longer be neutral or ambiguous with regard to the convictions, beliefs and practices that are favored by a specific ecclesial tradition and its institutions.

As stated, a dominant "feature" of the overall structure of Christian interactions concerns the harvesting and deployment of biblical quotations which contribute to the engagements concerning power relations and what Fairclough refers to as "ideological processes." For Fairclough and critical discourse analysist broadly, "ideology" is associated with those processes of discourse that serve to establish and maintain a status quote of socio-political structures which become so habitual that such discourse and arrangements are considered "natural." To think, behave, or believe otherwise would be "un-natural" if such thinking, behaving or believing is even possible within the confines of a totalizing socio-political culture.

It is my argument that the processes for constructing and competing for dominance among alternative movements and groups who identify themselves as Christian always concern the drawing, harvesting and incorporation of biblical quotations into their differing religious discourses. Intra-Christian competitions and conflicts are waged over and by means of quotations. And so the sense of quoting scripture among Christians concerns the competitive engagements in which quotations are deployed as strategic weapons in the embattled discourses among competing Christians.

The faithful engage one another in a battle of the quotes. Quotes serve as tactical weapons in an engagement in direct debate and confrontation. The harvesting of quotations serves as the manufacturing of weapons which utilize Christian scripture in engagements which seek to institute actions, force, power and even violence against opposing Christian socio-political sides, and establish and economy of religious advantages and disadvantages.

Despite differences within the various movements and ecclesial institutions that compete with one another as Christians, all competitors share in common the drawing and deploying of biblical quotations to legitimate discursive authority. The rhetorical use of biblical quotations is a shared procedure among most if not all contending parties who seek to forward their influence in power struggles and relations. The manifest differences between the competing movements and ecclesial institutions concern such things as the selection of phrases for harvesting and quoting, and the status, purpose and effective use of a quotation in a discourse. Oft times competing movements and ecclesial institutions are found to select the same phrase for harvesting and quoting. The quotation may contribute to significantly different discursive ventures in support of divergent if not competing institutions. Or in some instances the common quote exhibits similar status, purpose and effect in otherwise different meta-discursive ventures for divergent social and political ecclesial institutions.

Quoting a phrase from scripture for discursive purposes serves to re-write the script in coordination and correlation with one's social and political ecclesiastically strivings.

Once a side is established in their power and authority in relation to their competitors, the legacies of "correlation" concerning the arrangements of socio-political power and authority with a Christian discourse become naturalized. Those with competing sectarian Christian convictions, practices, institutions and societies are evaluated as seditious, unchristian if not anti-Christian. And so such drawn and deployed biblical quotes which contribute to the discursive ideology of a dominant socio-political authority, become naturalized features in the processes of a theo-political discourse.

Repetition is pervasive in discourse. And within a variety of different and often competing Christian discourses in their striving to influence, the repetitive feature of the discourse is the persistent and pervasive use of biblical quotations. When a "text" is reproduced and recited in part as a quote either in a text which incorporates the quote or when recited orally in a public presentation, the segment selected for repetition derives much of its "meaning" and "value" by virtue of being repeated as a unit abstracted out of its source and contextualized in the new script or in the performance. Thus, the sense of the phrase as quoted is drawn anew in relation with the discourse in which the quote is recited. For to recite is more than to simply repeat a phrase as deployed in a discourse. The Latin *recitāre* means to read out. Its root "*citāre*" (from the Indo-European root *keiə*) means to set in motion, often associated with a sense of to summon. To recite, as in to read out, possibly again suggests a rich semiotic play upon the sense of a sign which signifies something else or something more is an association of both source text (and all that implies) and the discourse in which the quotation comes to be recited. Thus, a discourse serves to read out the quotation from its source such that the quotation is set in motion beyond the page in the discursive recitation. The effective meaning and value of a phrase quoted is added to or changed in its use in the target discourse beyond the script. And so, the quoted material may be reevaluated and reinterpreted differently in the discourse from its occurrence in the source text. The influence of quoting thus serves to bring the influence of the discourse to bear on the sense of the quoted phrase material, which in turn affects the sense of the quoted phrase or sentences when read again in the source text. Quotations remain under the influence of the discourse so long as the discourse remains a dominant socio-cultural-political force.

In some instances, I argue, quoted phrase segments of a text as it appears in a subsequent work will come to represent or stand for the biblical text from which it was drawn, often without conveying any sense of the features or content of the quotation in relation to the sense of the source text. Thus, the influence of the discourse over the quoted phrase and the source text serves to cloak the sense of the quote in the cohesive relations of phrases and sentences in the source text. Such cloaking may render the full source text as functionally obsolete. For the scriptural *textus* once harvested fades from consideration, being replaced by a Christian discursive ideology that has harvested and operationalized what is found to be useful.

To read aloud an ancient Greek script requires the eloquent ancient reader to spend time with the manuscript in order to disentangle the continuous script so as to yield a reading which clearly articulated the wording and phrasing.⁶ Returning to 1 Corinthians 1:10–13, what is often missing in the English translation are the repetition of the particle δε which punctuates the quotations of self-belonging.

ΕΓΩ ΜΕΝ ΕΙΜΙ ΠΑΥΛΟΥ ΕΓΩ ΔΕ ΑΠΟΛΛΩ ΕΓΟ ΔΕ ΚΗΦΑ ΕΓΩ ΔΕ ΧΡΙΣΤΟΥ

I belong to Paul, I to Apollo, I to Cephas, I to Christ.

Note the presence of the Greek particle δε is in the second position of the second, third and fourth declaration of belonging to Apollos, Cephas and Christ. But the particle is not commonly translated. Nor is the use of the particle δε accounted for as regards what the particle conveys except by the use of the comma suggesting both a continuation of a line of thought and contrast between the declarations. Would it make a difference in how this chain of quotations would be read and understood in the context of the larger script if we were to attend to the information that the particle δε might convey an adversative stance towards the quotations as we read the text?

It is common to find that the effective reading of the script of quotations results in the first three declarations being assessed as expressive of the dissensions within the congregation while the fourth and final declaration, *I to Christ* is presented as almost credo, as a declaration which will unite the congregants in the same mind and the same judgment. "I belong to Christ" (Odell-Scott 2003, 32–47). Except there is a problem with this assessment of the value of the fourth self-declaration. For immediately there is a query evident in the syntax of the three-term phrase to follow.

---

6 Parkes notes in *Their Hands Before our Eyes* that "A book trade was operating in Rome from the first century BC. Cicero refers to a bookseller's stall or shop (*taberna libraria*) and to the punctuation marks (*notae librarirum*) that copyists inserted in texts copied for less experienced readers (or, perhaps, for those who read books aloud to others who could not read for themselves)" (Parkes: 2008: 3). The trade mentioned by Cicero, while apparently something of a novelty, suggests something of what was to come as the task of remastering the script became one of the tasks to be performed first by scribes often under the direction of the house guides or customs for style and punctuation of specific scriptoriums in the production of medieval manuscript copies, and later in the publishing houses which came to formalize styles and punctuation, and to exert enormous influence as to how biblical works in Greek or translation would be "re-mastered" under a publisher's technologies, techniques and formal style.

ΜΕΜΕΠΙΣΤΑΙ Ο ΧΡΙΣΤΟΣ

Has Christ divided himself?

I argue that in response to the four self-declarations of belonging, which are presented as four quotations which have been orally delivered by Chloes people to Paul, and are presented as reported in verses 10 and 11 as expressive of what congregants are saying and doing in the Rome-Corinth city church which is breeding division in the congregation or among the congregations, Paul engages in a direct forthright three-fold negative rhetorical critique.

ΛΕΥΩ ΔΕ ΤΟΥΤΟ ΟΤΙ ΕΚΑΣΤΟΣ ΥΜΩΝ ΛΕΓΕΙ ΕΓΩ ΜΕΝ ΕΙΜΙ ΠΑΥΛΟΥ ΕΓΩ ΔΕ ΑΠΟΛΛΩ ΕΓΟ ΔΕ ΚΗΦΑ ΕΓΩ ΔΕ ΧΡΙΣΤΟΥ

I mean this that each of you says I belong to Paul, I to Apollo, I to Cephas, I to Christ.

ΜΕΜΕΡΙΣΤΑΙ Ο ΧΡΙΣΤΟΣ ΜΝ ΠΑΥΛΟΣ ΕΣΤΑΥΡΩΘΗ ΥΠΕΡ ΥΜΩΝ Η ΕΙΣ ΤΟ ΟΝΟΜΑ ΠΑΥΛΟΥ ΕΒΑΠΤΙΣΘΗΤΕ

Has Christ divided himself? Was Paul crucified for you? Or were you baptized in the name of Paul?

Of course, there were clues leading up to and including the quotations of the second, third and fourth declarations that something was afoot. Each contained the particle δε which when employed in a letter, and in relationship to a quotation, may convey a sense that the author (Paul) is addressing the quotes and those who are being quoted, as adversarial. But this status is realized in Paul's reply to the quoted phrases. That is, Paul is marking the quotations (or possibly Paul's secretary is marking the quotations) with the particle δε to indicate that Paul is averse to their claims. His reply begins immediately following the self-declaration of I (δε) to Christ with his first target being those who claim some privileged sense of belonging to Christ. And following his negative rhetorical critical query concerning belonging to Christ, he follows with two interrogative negative rhetorical questions which target the first claim of belonging to Paul. The full range of Paul's critique centers on the sense of the phrase μεμερισται ο Χριστος at 1:13a (Odell-Scott 2003, 44–46). When presented as quote and reply in quick order, the nuances of the critique are apparent:

"I (δε) to Christ." Has Christ divided himself?
Did Christ allocate himself?
Did Christ distribute himself?

I offer the different senses of μεμερισται suggested by its root μεριζω, meaning to divide, allocate, distribute, bestow, assign. Thus, as I argued, μεμερισται as "a perfect periphrastically constructed middle voice" construction renders the question as to the subject dividing, allocation distribution, bestowing, and assigning the subject. The point being that in this adversative engagement introduced by the addition of the particle δε by Paul or by his scribe in the transcription, the negative query to follow calls into question the legitimacies of the privilege and advantage of anyone declaring "belonging" to Christ. But the sense of the particles added to the sequence of quoted declarations of belonging, as well as the nuances of the first negative rhetorical query concerning Christ distributing himself to those who declare belonging to him, are missed in the all too common discourses which draw upon the phrase "I (belong) to Christ" as a quotation of proper declared belief. Quoting the phrase of belonging to Christ at 1:12e, or more properly re-quoting the quotation at 1:12e as if it were credo would be to misunderstand the structure of the critical engagement and the sense of the quote copied by Paul in his epistolary reply as to misquote the passage as used by Paul (Odell-Scott 2003, 33–67).

As I have argued in *Paul's Critique of Theocracy*, the claim to belong to Christ quoted of someone in Corinth was probably not a declaration of belief, but a declaration of "belonging" to a household. Thus Paul's quoting and quick order interrogative reply was not a critique of a belief, but a critique of an expression of entitlement by virtue of being a member of Christ's household.

Conclusion

The sense of a quote occurs at a rather elementary level when a reader begins to identify that a phrase in a text may be quotable. The sense of a phrase *as* quotable, *as if* the phrase might be quotable, entails the reader imagining the phrase being quoted for a purpose, whether as expressive or aesthetic, or for a discursive purpose. To incorporate a quote in a discourse is to inscribe the scripture in the discourse for some "scripture-ive" purpose. Such quotations may be found to inscribe the text in a correlative engagement in which objects or artifacts or entities or events or action in the world (to name a few) are descripted (as in scripting the objects or artifacts or entities or events or actions with scripture). Such correlations operationalize quotations as inscriptive and descriptive such that something is being described with scripture (depending upon the conventions and codes).

THE SENSE OF QUOTING

Given the play with the sense of texture and tissue associated with the term text (*textus*), the question concerns to what degree is it necessary for the quote so harvested and deployed in a discourse to convey the sense of the quoted phrase as it occurred in the source text prior to harvesting. To what extent is the phrase as quoted liberated from the confines of its source tissue, a phrase left behind depleted and plundered? Is the script which has been so harvested reduced such that the harvesting by means of περικοπη is περι-λοπτας, as the laying waste of the source *textus* little more than the production waste in discursive manufacturing? The sense of a quote as harvested and deployed in a discourse is to effect, to exercise an effect which serves to influence the reader of one's work or the audience of one's presentation into which the quote is deployed.

A successful quotation of Christian scripture conveys a quality of meaning and authority *as a* quote in the context of a discourse in which the quotation is incorporated and exercises an effect. And so the quoted phrase is deployed by the one quoting so as to offer something more in the presentation. It is this something more of a quote that triggers further semiotic analysis.

The quotation of a phrase prepared and harvested from scripture is rarely employed in Christian discourse as simply a means of conveying simple content from the source. Quoting is not just neutral recycling of a phrase. Rather, often, maybe too often as I argue, the deployment of a pericope cut and drawn from Christian scriptures in being quoted signifies an authority which enriches the status and the power of the discursive venture for which the *textus* was mutilated in the production of quotes. Thus the incorporation of the quoted phrase is made sense of by the operational or procedural systems which come into play in the discourse. The content of the quoted scripture phrase in having been pericoped from the source script, having been relieved of its "context," the "frame" in which it occurred, and relieved as well of the codes which informed the sense of the phrase in the source script, is like the source *textus* from which it is drawn, mutilated in the process of harvesting. The phrase as trimmed out is thus manufactured and finished such that the "quote" fits and serves its purpose in the discursive venture. The fitting out of the quote serves to shape the quote such that it contributes to the articulation of the discourse. But the sense of content in the discursive context differs from the sense of the content of the phrase in the source text. In other words, quoted phrases rarely convey the code and conventions operating in the cohesive, coherent articulations of the source as they are placed and fitted into the discourse in which they are quoted.

The cohesiveness of the source *textus* is lost as the phrase is fitted out to be autonomous, as a phrase unbounded by the conditions and restraints of the source. Thus the quote *as* trimmed out from the script is deployed in the construction of a discourse and is re-contextualized, reframed and reconfigured *as* a quotation. Once woven into the target discourse the previously contextualized phrase in the source text is re-contextualized in a new *textus*. As a quotation, integrated in the discourse, the phrase no longer belongs to its source, but comes to belong in the discourse. The subsequent influence of the content of the phrase "as quoted" occurs in the discourse in which the phrase is rewritten and reframed.

And in this process the reframed quote no longer conveys the cohesiveness, coherence and/or the articulations of the source script from which it was harvested. For a quote *as* a quote is more or other than the phrase as woven in the source text. In being harvested from its source and deployed as a quote in a new discourse, the quoted phrase is hosted as a quote and so inhabits a new textual domain. As such, a quotation is deployed for discursive purposes which are not identical with the phrase as framed and configured in the source *textus*. At best "quoting" may convey *some* sense of the content from the source, some semblance of the source text. And at least, such quoting might at most or at best convey a family resemblance with the source (Wittgenstein). Otherwise a quote would not be a quote of another but simply a new phrase. But the quote, its semblance to the source text and the sense of the phrase in the source *textus*, are stripped of their encoding in order to be encoded anew in service to the discourse.

To simply repeat the source text in totality without cultivating and harvesting quotations is not to quote the text but to "copy" the text, to "read" the text, or "recite" the work. Thus a quote is often at best little more than a semblance of a segment of the discursive source *textus* which has been recoded. And as such, the recoded phrase is not the same as the phrase encoded in the source.

I argue that the identification, harvesting and deployment of scriptural quotations in a subsequent discourse often has to do with the identified phrase as a useful quotation which the reader of the scriptures seeks to draw into the writer or orator's composing or presenting. But the identification and harvesting of such quotes from the source, which are deployed in a subsequent discourse does not convey, and need not and most often does not convey, much of the sense of the cohesiveness, coherence and articulations of the source discourse in order to exercise an effect and influence as a quote in the discourse.

And this leads me to argue that the status of a quotation is determined by a phrase being quoted in the context of the discourse in which it is incorporated. The legacies of a specific phrase being quoted often, repeated as an integral element which is articulated in a cohesive and coherent common discourse, is the means by which the content of the quote becomes naturalized in the narratives of a widely held social discourse. And, given the legacy of the quoted material enjoying the privileged status of an often recycled quotation from scripture for specific purposes which enforce a society's discursive convictions and commitments, the quote serves to confirm by association the authority of the source from which it was drawn but under the authority of the society and the discourse in which the "quote" serves to signify the "source."

Christian scriptures are the naturalized principle source of quotations whose influences lace through all manner of Christian life and institutions. But knowledge of the source texts which are venerated as scripture are for the most part little more than an acquaintance with specific drawn quotes whose efficacy in legacies of institutional discourse often have little to do with the sense of the quoted phrase or verse as regards the cohesive script from which it was harvested. The effectiveness of Christian scriptures is present in the piecemeal rewriting and rescoring of quotations in discursive ventures whereby the quote is correlated.

We have followed out to what might be a logical conclusion regarding Parkes's hypothesis that the ancient Greek manuscripts provided a "neutral" script for readers who both cultivated and produced quotations, and who by means of adding their own marks of punctuation and style served in no small measure to re-fabricate the resource or as I have suggested, to rescore the text. But there is a critical problem as regards Parkes "neutral" script hypothesis which I have touched on but not explored. And this critical problem concerns the semiotic analytics of an ancient Greek *textus*. In terms of both social and political context of the script, by means of semiotic pragmatic analysis, and by means of *textus* semiotic analysis, the ancient Greek manuscripts composed and copied in all capital letters of the Greek alphabet in a continuous script without spacing to separate words and paragraphs, and with no punctuation, were already, always and nevertheless structured *textus* which was appointed (though not punctuated) by the use of "particles". These particles scattered throughout the manuscripts were largely later ignored given that they made no sense in the script as "signs" or better on Augustine's terms, "words" as signs. Not being words the status of the Greek particles persisted as conundrums which were either read out of the text, or translated as words. And so failing to fulfill the expectations that all that mattered in the text was the wording and the syntactical sense made possible by Greek grammatical functions of the wording, the particles were "nothing." Or, under the persuasion of such conceptual operations and the readings which became route and naturalized, the particles were read over, glossed over, and so became invisible to readers well trained and well-rehearsed.

Part 3. Manufacturing Plainer Passages

Orthodox Quotations: Augustine on Sentential Order

It is commonly assessed that at some mid-point in the last decade of the fourth century, Augustine began to write *On Christian Teaching* (*De Doctrina Christiana*), completing Chapters 1, 2 and most of 3, then setting the work aside for some thirty years before returning to complete Chapter 3 and write Chapter 4. In the beginning pages of Chapter 3, written around 395 CE, Augustine writes

> When it is literal usages that make scripture ambiguous, we must first of all make sure that we have not punctuated or articulated the passage incorrectly. Once close consideration has revealed that it is uncertain how a passage should be punctuated and articulated, we must consult the rule of faith, as it is perceived through the plainer passages of the scriptures and the authority of the church. But if both interpretations, or indeed all of them (supposing that there are several sides to the ambiguity) sound compatible with the faith, then it remains to consult the context—the preceding and following passages, which surround the ambiguity—in order to determine which of the several meanings that suggest themselves is supported by it, and which one lends itself to acceptable combinations with it.
>
> AUGUSTINE 3:3–4

Augustine's comment regarding the reader's punctuating or articulating the passage correctly or incorrectly expresses the developing status of the nascent desire and ambiguous development of codes of sentential order and the use of a graphic sign to denote in the script how to distinguish one sentence from the next by fitting out the script with the use of a mark of distinction (the period). Well towards the end of the first and the beginning of the second millennium the history and application of punctuation was still new and under development such that non-lettered markings were added at the discretion of readers with the meaning of such markings more or less idiosyncratic both in terms of the characters sometimes employed and the purpose for the placement of the character

Just a few lines earlier in chapter 3, Augustine instructed readers of scripture to examine the manuscripts so as to ensure that the verse was correctly copied, and to assess how the phrase fit in its immediate placement in the script. Augustine then turns to an example in the Prologue of John.

> Consider now the following examples. The well-known heretical punctuation (Latin: *Illa haeretica distinctio*) 'In the beginning was the Word, and the Word was with God, and there was God' (Or, simply "God was.") (Latin: *In principio erat verbum, et verbum erat apud Deum, et Deus erat*) giving a different sense in what follows ('this word was in the beginning with God', Latin: *Verbum hoc erat in principio apud Deum*) refuses to acknowledge that the Word was God. But this is to be refuted by the rule of faith, which lays down for us the equality of the members of the Trinity, and so we should say "and the Word was God" (Latin: *et Deus erat verbum*), and then go on, "this was in the beginning with God" (Latin: *hoc erat in principio apud Deum*).
> AUGUSTINE 3:5

Note, that the reader's choice in pointing the script produces a different configuration of sentences. The result of the different location of the pointing of the script with the production of different sentences is that the "*Illa haeretica distinctio,*" the heretical distinction or punctuation produces on Augustine's reckoning theological heretical sentences. And the reason this is a concern is that the construction of heretical sentences might then be drawn upon as heretical *sententiae*, as quotations which support heretical Christian belief and convictions. What matters for Augustine is that the questionable heretical pointing forecloses the possibility that the verse articulates the phrase "In the beginning was the word ... *and the Word was God.*" The heretical punctuation severed "word" and "God" into different sentences.

> In the beginning was the Word, and the Word was with God, and God was. The Word was in the beginning with God

The distinction thus rendered the valued quotation asunder. What is at stake for Augustine was the status of orthodox theological decisions in support of a "Trinitarian" theology and an "incarnational" Christology, both of which drew upon the quote bore by the phrase in the Prologue that "the logos was God." The alternative pointing of the script supported a different theology in which the Word and God are not so conjoined. The Word was with God, even with God in the beginning. But the Word was not God. At issue over where to point the script is which sentences will be confirmed and which phrase can be harvested as effective quotes from scripture in support for one's Christianity.

Punctuation and articulation of scripture must for Augustine, serve the "rule of faith" such that the settled matters by authority of the Council's declarations are supported. To produce alternative sentences by pointing and articulating which in turn provide the reader alternative "quotations" would counter the rule of faith and vacate the quotations as drawn from the Gospel of John in support of Orthodox Christianity.

The question over where to draw a distinction and so "cut" the continuous script with the insertion of a point and a pause, so as to divide up the continuous script into units, served to cultivate the script in such a way as to influence what would flourish and be made available for harvesting. And likewise, what would be cut off or so pruned could result is some harvestable fruit for an orthodox reading withering away and perishing. The choice was itself a battle over how the text could be harvested for useful quotations. And in turn, whose quotes would represent the Gospel of John and which formulation of Christianity would come to enjoy authority.

Augustine warns that "we must first of all make sure that we have not punctuated or articulated the passage incorrectly" (Augustine 3.3). Augustine is referring to the fact that the manuscripts of Christian scripture, as we discussed earlier, are like all other texts written and copied in Greek and Latin at the time, free of punctuation and stylized spacing, and written in all capital letters in a continuous script. The criteria forwarded by Augustine as to how to assess correctly the establishment of sentential order by means of the use of the period is expected to bring forth the sense of a passage such that the order serves to bring clarity to the script.

Augustine continues, "Once close consideration has revealed that it is uncertain how a passage should be punctuated and articulated, we must consult the rule of faith, as it is perceived through the plainer passages of scripture and the authority of the church" (Augustine 3.3). Now by these standards Augustine acknowledges that some passages remain ambiguous and so may be differently punctuated in keeping with different senses of a passage's articulation. Thus, when the sense of a passage remains unclear, then the reader should council the rule of faith. The "rule of faith" is to be consulted "through the plainer passages of scripture and the authority of the church." The "rule of faith" is thus informed by the "plainer passages" and "the authority of the church." It is my judgment that what Augustine orchestrated was the cultivation of a plainer passage by fitting out the script with appointments so as to craft "plainer passages" in service to the rule of faith as established by the church.

It was not till later in the first millennium of the Common Era that spacing between words in the Greek manuscripts were introduced. Various parochial systems for demarcating the script were devised and used for a time, but these marks and their supportive codes were not concerned as it were with the same task for punctuation. That is, in many instances the use of punctuation was used to provide how to perform the script as if it were some hybrid of song and reading so as to effect an eloquent performance of the scriptures. Thus decisions were made by copyists and editors regarding the structures of a text into paragraphs with respect to the "perceived" content and articulation of the prose. The demarcation of paragraph order is evident in biblical copies as early as Codex Sinaiticus where the first line of each paragraph was marked beginning slightly to the left of the margin line for the body of the column text with the last of the paragraph concluding and leaving space on the line between the end of the paragraph and the right margin. The decision for such structuring was apparently orchestrated by the scribe who also served as something of a "production" editor of the composition regarding the matter of paragraph structure.

The focus of Augustine's exploration of the use of signs and the art of reading scripture concerns his attention to so fit out or score the script with sentential order that it supports the production of *sententiae* (phrases for quoting) from the script which are in keeping with the rule of faith. The harvesting of *sententiae* from the continuous script was an important and sometimes difficult endeavor. Once a reader deciphered how best to read the script such that it supported the reader's purposes, it was not uncommon for a reader to mark the manuscript with the use of a point. Readers were for the most part limited to only "pointing" their own script. These demarcations were the result of the interactions between a reader and the wording of a script often with the purpose for the reader being to more easily locate and quote again some *sententiae* which had earlier been harvested for personal or public use, whether for edification, liturgical or rhetorical value. In classical rhetoric and the training of elite students in the art of persuasion, the integration of a quote in one's own work such that the quote was in keeping with the use and status of the phrase in the source text was of little or no concern. It was as if the purpose for reading was to provide the reader useful quotations for his own purposes, rhetorical or otherwise.

Augustine makes much of *pronuntiatio* (which commonly means pronunciation or delivery) as another means in addition to the use of sentential distinction by means of punctuation for resolving the ambiguities in scripture when the wording in the passages are found to be ambiguous. Augustine offered several strategies for resolving such ambiguity often drawing upon the work of Cicero. He recommended that the reader insure that the manuscript was a good copy before reviewing the ambiguous phrase or sentence in the larger context, considering what preceded and what followed. And so, it was at this point when a phrase continued to be ambiguous that Augustine recommended that the reader take into consideration how best to divide up the script or how best to perform the proclamation of the script. That is, if dividing the script into different configurations failed to resolve the ambiguity and to render a reading in compliance with the rule of faith, then considering options for how best to perform the script aloud employing techniques of oral eloquent performance might serve to draw out ways of articulating the script which might resolve the ambiguity.

These endeavors of drawing upon the wording in the script and seeking clarity as to how the script might convey a sense of division and/or articulation in performance so as to resolve ambiguities as to the content and sense of the scriptures. But these endeavors are influenced by differential codes of Christian thought and practice. I argue that the "plainer passages" are the product of manufacturing the continuous script.

In Augustine's dealing with the prologue of the Gospel of John and the problem of punctuation of the script belies the notion as regards sentential stability and coherence. As Augustine argued, the sense of the script in this instance is ambiguous if not unstable and may come to be so appointed and pronounced as to yield different sentences altogether. His point, "the well-known heretical punctuation" produced the following reading:

> In the beginning was the word, and the word was with God and God was. This word was in the beginning with God.

This heretical reading and the decision as to the punctuation proceeds in such a way that the placement of the period does not disrupt the word order of the Greek script. The Greek script of John 1: 1–2 reads:

> ΕΝ ΑΡΧΗ ΗΝ Ο ΛΟΓΟΣ ΚΑΙ Ο ΛΟΓΟΣ ΗΝ ΠΡΟΣ ΤΟΝ ΘΕΟΝ ΚΑΙ ΘΕΟΣ ΗΝ
>
> In (the) beginning was the word and the word was with the God and God was.
>
> Ο ΛΟΓΟΣ ΟΥΤΟΣ ΗΝ ΕΝ ΑΡΧΗ ΠΡΟΣ ΤΟΝ ΘΕΟΝ
>
> This word was in (the) beginning with the God.

That is, the heretical punctuation followed the Greek word order common in available manuscripts and offered a grammatically correct reading of the script that served to foreclose other options for readers who might wish to exercise a reader's choice to articulate the script by considering alternative syntactic word associations. On the orthodox reading the period is not placed at the end of 1b but placed after "the word" (ὁ λόγος), thus resulting in the following sentential order which rendered the following.

ΕΝ ΑΡΧΗ ΗΝ Ο ΛΟΓΟΣ ΚΑΙ Ο ΛΟΓΟΣ ΗΝ ΠΡΟΣ ΤΟΝ ΘΕΟΝ ΚΑΙ ΘΕΟΣ ΗΝ Ο ΛΟΓΟΣ.

In (the) beginning was the word and the word was with the God and the word was God.

ΟΥΤΟΣ ΗΝ ΕΝ ΑΠΧΗ ΠΡΟΣ ΤΟΝ ΘΕΟΝ.

It was in (the) beginning with the God.

The issues concerning a fluidity or ambiguity as regards Greek word order may sound odd to a modern reader who is accustomed to the word order of their native modern language providing some indication of the sense of a phrase. But for an ancient reader, working with scripts which were "neutral" as we have noted, and for whom word order as well as sentential order were to be determined in significant measure by the reader, the choice to punctuate the text at the point selected against the "rule of faith" and the choice to reorder the words in the production of sentential order and punctuate the text differently in keeping with the "rule of faith" would not have been regarded as a grammatical *faux pas*. Both would be reasonable. Both would make grammatical sense. Both readings introduce marks of distinction to differentiate sentential order which respect Greek grammatical elements in the phrasing. Both account for the syntax of the individual terms in play. But the content produced by these differing articulations yield very different claims.

The debate concerned the differences between the drawing of sentences by Arian Christians and Orthodox Christians. Augustine asserted that the alternative Arian distinction of the script is to be refuted by the rule of faith which denotes for Augustine the decisions reached concerning the establishment of Trinitarian theology which maintains that the logos which was incarnate in Jesus was God and with God in the beginning. In other words, the Logos was from the beginning not made by God, but was and with God in the holy Trinity. Arian theology maintained that the logos while with God in the beginning of creation was not God, and exists by virtue of God having created the logos.

And why does this matter? What was at stake for the Arians was the sovereignty of God as singular. For the logos to be on a par with God would be to compromise Arian monotheism which was a cornerstone in their theological discourse. What was at stake for Augustine as an orthodox Christian was the authority of the church to settle matters of faith as regards theological and Christological controversies, and the meaning and purpose of Christian scriptures. Scripture was to serve the rule of faith as determined by the churches, and to provide witness and teachings of the rule of faith. For Augustine, faith is qualified as the right faith as expressed in his time as the rule of faith as established by the Ecumenical Councils which he would argue had the authority to determine orthodoxy. Given that the rule of faith was a matter settled by means of convention to which those who participated and joined forces, the majority established the rule of faith as the product of a political process under the sovereignty of the Councils. And that sovereignty was in some instance ambiguous and in other instances forthright and plain, at the pleasure of the Emperor.

While Augustine was alive and active in the life of the church, the rule of faith as he defined it was still under contest. In fact, just a few years after the death of Augustine the fourth ecumenical council held in Ephesus reversed some decided rules of faith by previous councils (albeit by questionable means). A subsequent Ecumenical Council was convened on order of the Emperor and actually conducted its business at the Emperor's estate located in Chalcedon under the watchful eye of the Emperor. The subsequent creed issued by the council incorporated clearly Aristotelian influences into the two natures Christology. Thus, in the fifth Ecumenical Council the rule of faith possibly came under the undue influence of the Emperor's representatives (Odell-Scott 1991, 83–91).

The reason making the right choices for how to appoint and pronounce a script mattered because there was no clear demarcation on how to appoint and perform the continuous script provided in John 1:1 & 2. How the script was to be fitted out by use of periods to distinguish sentential units produces different sentential orders to be drawn from the text and determine what could be quoted in support of alternative coherent systems of belief. Given the association of the church with Imperial power, the Church sought to exert an authority sanctioned by the emperors to determine by decree what is orthodox and what is heretical. If the script can be differentiated into different sentences from the convention which Augustine defends, and which supports the quotes drawn from John in the discourse of the church, then the cohesion of the *textus* as sentenced, may serve to undermine and oppose Christian orthodoxy.

As regards the identification and application of drawn *sententiae* from scripture, Augustine's concern and persistent defense of the rule of faith may be more in keeping with an understanding of "correlation" mentioned earlier. That is, the questions confronting Augustine—questions with nuanced urgency concerning finitude, mortality, ethical behavior, etc., could all have been the questions to which he sought to establish and protect by means of his establishment of the sentential order of the script. Thus, Augustine's scoring of the script occasioned by contesting theological discourses competing for influence in Christianity, was an outcome of how he correlated the contests and questions of his day with answers provided by scripture as crafted by his application of appointments such that the sentential order supported his answers.

And, the same was true for the Arians. That is, the questions confronting the Arians—questions with nuanced urgency concerning finitude, mortality, ethical behavior, etc., could all have been the questions to which they sought to establish and protect by means of their seeking to determine their sentential order of the script in order to protect their pericopes. Thus, Augustine's scoring of the script ran counter to their own cause as they sought to correlate the contests and questions of the day with answers provided by scripture as crafted by their application of appointments such that the sentential order supported their venerated quotations harvested in answer to the questions they entertained.

Given the limited repertory of graphic markings to distinguish sentential fitting and the nuances of grammar, Augustine would turn to the art of a public reading of the text aloud as performance, as oration, to discern how to play the text, how to play the recording of the script, and so rely upon rhetorical codes which inform the performer. Thus by means of performance, the reader may discern how to eloquently perform a script such that in play, a sense of the script is released or created in performance. The judgment as to how best to understand the script may require the ability of the reader to discern how best to fit out the script into a sentential order and to then by means of an engaged interaction with the phrasing which draws upon the sensibilities of the script for dramatic performance or the reader's trained sensibilities and techniques so as to discern what phrasing in the script is suggestive for the imaginative performance which exhibits in performance the possible textures and meanings associated by sound and pronunciation and articulation.

It would appear that Augustine is not purposing that readers exhibit a flat footed, tone deaf manner while reading, but that they perform the reading of the script such that one might upon hearing think through and make decisions as to what is a plainer or ambiguous meaning, without succumbing to a notion that by plainer Augustine meant dumber. What Augustine articulates in his engagement with Romans 8 and 9, was to value the reader who seeks to play the script as suggestive of an oration to be performed. So on Augustine's semiotic approach, what the limited markings available could not inform the reader to do would be augmented by a reader who received a formal rhetorical education and possessed the ability to perform the text with oratory eloquence.

Given that Augustine only had the period to work with in marking the text, the point served only to demarcate a sentence and so served in fitting out the script with periods such that a sentential order was installed in keeping with the potential structures as identified and marked by Augustine. But, working with how to pronounce or perform the script in light of its potential articulations or how to distinguish units in light of how it might best be proclaimed, provided options for Augustine to overcome the limitations which only the deployment of a period provided. Lacking codes and signs for marking a script such that more advanced and nuanced articulations could be indicated, Augustine was forced to resort to performance informed by the art and skill of rhetorical training and oratory eloquence without the available use of more sophisticated signs for scoring such performance.

So, what is lost given the ill-equipped techniques and technologies of writing at the time? True, the alphabetical marks on a page presented the spelled-out sounds of the wording dictated by the author which in a reflective grammar may convey to those skilled in the language how to decode a sense of the script as a performance which always proceeds procedurally. For acting and oration proceed by means of methods and techniques. Thus, being spelled and sounded out, the printed words could or might, upon being performed well, repeat both what was said and how it was said when captured and mastered by a scribe.

Quoting a Quote and the Question of a Plainer Passage
The Case of Male Celibacy

We return to what Augustine wrote in early pages of chapter 3 of *On Christian Teaching* which we discussed at the beginning of the previous chapter.

> When it is literal usages that make scripture ambiguous, we must first of all make sure that we have not punctuated or articulated the passage incorrectly. Once close consideration has revealed that it is uncertain how a passage should be punctuated and articulated, *we must consult the rule of faith, as it is perceived through the plainer passages of the scriptures and the authority of the church.* But if both interpretations, or indeed all of them, if there are several sides to the ambiguity, sound compatible with the faith, then it remains to consult the context—the preceding and following passages, which surround the ambiguity—in order to determine which of the several meanings that suggest themselves is supported by it, and which one lends itself to acceptable combinations with it.
>
> AUGUSTINE 3: 3–4

The sentence in Augustine's work that is italized above may be appointed differently, thus serving to influence the relation of the status of "the rule of faith" which is to be consulted as perceived through the plainer passages of the scriptures and the authority of the church. For it would appear on one reading that the rule of faith is perceived through the plainer passages and the authority of the church. But what comes when what is "a plainer passage" conflicts with the authority of the church?

An early example of Paul's epistles being harvested for pericopes drawn in support of a contested position under debate among competing parties in Christianity at the time also includes evidence that the same work by Paul was being harvested for pericopes in support of the opposing side in the debate. Drawn conflicting pericopes from the collection of epistles written by Paul to the Corinthian congregation were deployed as if they were tactical rhetorical weapons, with each side contending that their position was warranted by the Apostle as evident in their quotation. The debate considered the opposing claims concerning whether a man seeking to be righteous and holy must abstain from heterosexual relations with his wife. The author of the text *Monogamy*, is the famed if not infamous Quintus Septimius Florens Tertullianus, (c. 160–c. 225 CE) who is otherwise know by his anglicized name Tertullian. Tertullian quotes Paul in *Monogamy* (210–220 CE).

> "Yes", you say, "but the right to marry still remains". True, it does remain and with what restrictions it remains we shall see later on. It is already partially abrogated, however in so far as continence is said to be preferable. "It *is good*," he says, *"for a man not to touch a woman"* Therefore, it is bad to touch one. For nothing is opposed to the "good" except the "bad".
> TERTULLIAN, 73

It's important to note that Tertullian is replying in *Monogamy* to someone who has defended the position that Christian men and women need not refrain from marriage or marital relations out of fear of doing what is bad. It is important to further note that Tertullian quotes his adversary and the adversary's use of quotes harvested from Paul's letter to the Corinthians, not because Tertullian wants to defend his quoted adversary or the adversary's use of the drawn quote. Rather, Tertullian quotes his advisory in order to make clear the position Tertullian wants to directly and forthrightly critique. Tertullian quotes the position of his contemporary and notes the use of quotes drawn from the same letter to the Corinthians by Paul that he will also quote. In fact, it is clear in *Monogamy* that both Tertullian and the defender of Christian marriage are appealing to drawn quotes from roughly the same section of the First Letter to the Corinthians which in later centuries would be identified as Chapter 7.

So here we have evidence of what I refer to as dueling quotations or as one of the earliest surviving examples of a Christian rhetorical battle of the quotes. So we find Tertullian quoting someone who declares that the right to marry is allowed by the Apostle to which Tertullian then turns and argues the contrary position aided by his drawing a quote from the same source as his opponent. "It is good for a man not to touch a woman." The presumption is that the quoted verse could on Tertullian's account not be any plainer.

Several centuries later, Jerome writes in *Against Jovinianus* around 393, repeating the quote reiterated much of Tertullian's argument defending male heterosexual abstinence or continence in the pursuit of male consecration.

> "It is good," he says, "for a man not to touch a woman." If it is good not to touch a woman, it is bad to touch one: for there is no opposite to goodness but badness. But if it be bad and the evil is pardoned, the reason for the concession is to prevent worse evil. But surely a thing which is only allowed because there may be something worse has only a slight degree of goodness ... We must notice the Apostle's prudence. He did not say, it is good not to have a wife: but, it is good not to touch a woman: as though there were danger even in the touch: as though he who touched her, would not escape from her who "hunteth for the precious life," who causeth the young man's understanding to fly away.
>
> JEROME 1: §7

First, it is important to note that I do not claim that Tertullian and Jerome miscopied the verse concerning it being good for a man not to touch a woman. I concur that the verse cited is a negative evaluation of a man having heterosexual contact with a woman. The quoted verse is as it appears in the source texts in Greek and the allusion to heterosexual touching is explicit. So far so good!

Tertullian's comment proceeded by further drawing another quote from the chapter at 1 Corinthians 7:29 where the Apostle declares:

> I mean, brothers and sisters, the appointed time has grown short; from now on, let even those who have wives be as though they had none.

Tertullian draws out the last phrase of the longer verse at 7:29, "let even those who have wives be as though they had none" and associates it with the earlier phrase "Good (it is) for a man not to have contact with a woman" at 1 Cor. 7:1 as providing "evidence" from the letter of the Apostle Paul in support of his own position that even married couples who remain "married" should seek a consecrated union as Christians without desire and therefore abstain from sexual contact with one another. The purpose for quoting the text was to draw out quotes in the production of a concatenation of scriptural pericopes to provide evidence in support of what both Tertullian and later Jerome present as a foregone conclusion and thereby affirm that their position concerning sexual abstinence is biblical and forthrightly authorized by the Apostle Paul.

Jerome goes so far as to contend that being married is simply not good. Marriage is just less evil than other options. Beginning with the first clause of verse 2, Jerome has Paul's reply begin with an argument in which marriage serves to counter the propensity for "πορνειας" often translated as fornication. Verse 2 ("Because of πορνειας each man should have his own wife and each woman her own husband") is associated with verse 9 ("For it is better to marry than to burn") such that marriage simply provides an outlet for sexual desire and satisfaction which reduces the possibility of πορνειας or illicit behavior. But even sexual contact by a husband and wife was not counted as a "good" by Jerome, but just as less evil than the excesses of unbridled sexual promiscuity. Jerome offered an exaggerated view of the physical power of the touch of a woman, maintaining that it is the physical touch that is evil because the touch of a woman, even the physical contact of a husband and a wife, can never be good. Jerome's analogy is that as he who touches fire is instantly burned, so for a man to touch a woman is to come under the influence or to be possessed by the touch. For a woman is presented by Jerome as if she were a predator who hunts for man in order to take a man's precious life as he loses his own mind. For Jerome, a man seduced into the clutches of a woman will lead to his ruin, his desecration.

In the history of Christianity, Tertullian and Jerome are often accredited as the architects in the instituting of the separation of women and men in church, and the move to establish a celibate, all male leadership in Christianity. And a corner stone of the edifice of an all celibate male clergy set by Tertullian and Jerome was quarried from 1 Corinthians, Chapter 7, verse 1b, as if the phrase was cut round from its source and trimmed out as an autonomous declaration by the Apostle. And so, if Tertullian and Jerome correctly copy the phrase "It is good for a man not to touch a woman" as it appears in the various manuscripts of Paul's letter, the reader might wonder why am I making such a fuss over the fact that Tertullian and Jerome correctly quote the verse?

Clearly, on the grounds established some century later by Augustine, Tertullian and Jerome have clearly discerned the rule of faith by means of the use of a plainer passage of scripture which is also authorized by the Church. But, there is a complication. And, it's a rather obvious complication. To put it bluntly, it is a simple complication. If you read a good copy of a half-way decent translation of the text of 1 Corinthians, Chapter 7, verse 1, you will read something along the lines of the following:

> Now concerning the matter about which you wrote, "It is good for a man not to touch a woman".

The phrase "It is good for a man to not touch a woman" is not part of a simple sentence or a straightforward declaration by Paul. Translators of the Greek text to modern English or into any other modern western language for that matter, mark that the phrase "It is good for a man to not touch a woman" as a "quote" which Paul introduces as having been drawn out of a letter addressed to him from the Corinthians. Paul writes that he is now considering "the matter about which you wrote." Could he have been any plainer in his introduction about the source of the phrase to follow? Quote marks are inserted by publishers at the beginning of the quoted phrase following the introduction to mark the opening of the quote and at the conclusion of the phrase to mark the close of the quote. Sometimes when the text is read aloud publicly the punctuation marks added to the printed text by the publishers are translated as parenthetical words.

> Now concerning the matter about which you wrote
> (Open quote) "It is good for a man not to touch a woman". (Close quote)

Or a public reader might simply indicate the presence of quotation marks by raising their hands and employing their pointer and middle fingers together indicate a marking of what they are saying by adding air quotations marks (not unlike strumming air guitar). At this point it should be noted again that the early Greek manuscripts of the letters of Paul, like all ancient Greek writings, do not include punctuation.

> ΠΕΡΙ ΔΕ ΩΝ ΕΓΡΑΨΑΤΕ ΚΑΛΟΝ ΑΝΘΡΩΠΩ ΓΥΝΑΙΚΟΣ ΜΗ ΑΠΤΕΣΘΑΙ
>
> Concerning (δὲ) which wrote good man woman not to touch

Punctuation and styles of spacing to express the grammar and articulation of a written work were in such a nascent stage of development by the first century, were not fully developed as a system, nor where such signs and codes in operation in any board sense. Early attempts to establish the use of a systematic manner for punctuation had in fact faded with the centuries. None attained widespread use and compliance. And with each attempt often following a time when little or no practice of punctuation attained more than provincial use, new systems emerged sometimes drawing upon previous graphic marks and sometimes associating the marks with the sense of articulation once ascribed by earlier conventions.

Returning to our quote from 1 Cor. 7:1, the reason for the verses being marked as a quote in modern print produced translations is that readers clearly understand that the source of the phrase is not Paul the apostle who is the author of the letter. Rather, Paul has selected a phrase to be quoted from a letter received from the congregation in Corinth which he introduces and incorporates into his own reply. Paul is explicit in his introduction. "Now concerning the matter about which you wrote...." Paul is quoting someone or others from Corinth who declared that it is good for a man to not have sexual relations with a woman. The introduction to the quote ("Now concerning the matter about which you wrote") is Paul's lead-in where he identifies in the wording of his epistles that the next topic to which he will reply concerns their claim which he forthwith quotes.

Given the content of the verse at 7:1a, the introduction is rather straightforward that the much-quoted verse in support of celibacy is a verse which Paul quoted. For modern readers of the text in translation and rescored in the use of the punctuated quotation marks, to open and close the phrase in 7:1b serves with quotation marks to inform the reader as to the status of the phrase as a quote which Paul incorporated into his own reply to the Corinthians. The use of the marks of punctuation are established conventions of reading and production. And the codes which govern the addition of quotation marks in a text are used and understood by writers, publishers and readers alike as normal signs which convey the status of the phrase as read and as agreed upon by readers such that so marked as a quotation for the reader the possibility that the script so quoted may articulate other moves to come. For the introduction simply notes that what is to come is a quotation but does not prepare the reader in advance for the sense of the quote within the *textus* of the epistle.

This is pretty simple stuff for the reader who has mastered the modern arts and skills of reading and writing. This level of mastery is attained by most students while attending modern elementary school. The elementary mastery of reading and understanding the alphabet, the words composed of the alphabet, non-alphabetical graphic marks of punctuation, and the spacing between words and the spacing of a page into paragraphs are all part of our modern elementary education of grammar.

So this is pretty simple, for us. Tertullian and Jerome draw and harvest a pericope so as to quote a phrase from Paul's letter to the Corinthians in their own work, but they do not declare that they are quoting a verse quoted by the apostle from the Corinthians. Someone or more probably a group in the Corinthian congregation declared a claim. But the semiotic question concerns what was their claim that was quoted by Paul. Was it as presented by Tertullian and Jerome that "it was good for a man not to touch a woman." And those who held the position, or those who disagreed with the position, or those who wanted to further explore the position, maybe quoted the declaration in their missive addressed and delivered to Paul in order to have Paul respond to the claim. They wanted to know what Paul thought about sexual abstinence as a means for attaining male consecration. Or whether a married man who maintained marital relations with his wife would no longer be considered consecrated given their sexual relations. We don't know if the phrase originated with someone in Corinth or if the Corinthians who proposed the declaration possibly for discussion in the congregation and repeated it to Paul were in turn also quoting someone else. As we stated earlier, tracing out the historical lineages of the discourse concerning heterosexual "touching" or relations as the means by which a man seeking consecration is desecrated by a woman, is not the concern of this study. (To explore this topic further, see Elizabeth Clark's work on *Reading Renunciation*.) What does concern our inquiry is that whoever declared the claim in Corinth, and whoever penned the letter or note to Paul remain anonymous in Paul's reply. And the text from which Paul drew out the quote has passed like so many other occasional written notes or messages generated over the centuries. It passed into dust. All that remains of the "text" addressed to Paul, a text which passes untitled and unattributed except as the matter written to Paul from Corinth, is the phrase which he quoted back to the Corinthians in his reply. We do not know all of the matters written to Paul or the source of these matters other than they came from the Corinthian congregation. We don't know if Paul correctly copied the matter raised or adequately represented the raised question, issue or position. For our only means of retrieving the exchange is by way of the letters of Paul which allude to the correspondence and apparently quotes from the now lost letter. So our evidence of what the Corinthians wrote for Paul to consider or conveyed in their missive is now, and has been for centuries, irretrievable except as quoted recycled phrasing presented in Paul's discursive reply.

All we have addressed at this point is the simple status of a much quoted "plainly stated phrase" (ala Augustine) as harvested as early as Tertullian for the purpose of supporting a discourse which champions male sexual abstinence in keeping with an institutionalization of a theocracy in which celibate males may enjoy the advantages of hierarchal authority in the Church as consecrated men to the exclusion of non-celibate males and all women (celibate or not).

What we have not considered at this point is the extent to which Tertullian and Jerome scored and remastered the text such that they insured the survival of the phrase for harvesting as an autonomous quote to be deployed in their discourse. We have not considered the questions concerning where or not to conclude the quotation at the established termination of the phrase as judged by Tertullian, Jerome and company. The beginning of the quotation is clearly evident in the syntax of the introduction to the quotation from Corinth. But where does the plainly phrased sentence concerning that it is good for a man not to touch a woman conclude or end, and where does Paul's response to this explicitly quoted phrase which introduced the topic for discussion begin?

So, we return again to the *sententiae* identified, harvested by means of pericope and deployed by Tertullian and Jerome in the establishment of Christian ecclesiastical theocracy in which social and political leadership is to be exercised exclusively in an all-male hierarchy in which men must make and apparently keep vows of celibacy. The beginning of Paul's harvested quote is found to be explicit given the introduction in verse 7:1a. But there is an ambiguity concerning the terminus of Paul's quotation of the phrase. This ambiguity is not evident in the classical and common reading of the text because the practice proposed as early as Tertullian and established by Jerome that the quotation in its entirety is as quoted by both authors: it is good for a man not to touch a woman. Their determination of the sentential order, the framing of the quoted phrase proved useful for their own discourse. But a complication concerns the status of the clause which follows their establishment of the sentential integrity of the quotation. For their punctuation of the script serves to differentiate the quotation and establish Paul's reply as beginning with the next clause.

The question as I see it is this: Was the subsequent clause also part of the quote which Paul harvested from a Corinthian missive and quoted in his reply? Or is the subsequent clause Paul's introduction of his response to the quoted material from Corinth?

The classical quotation only concerns the phrase at 7:1b. The practice of quoting the phrase may have influenced how the script was subsequently punctuated, such that the script was so divided that verse 1b was seen as complete. Thus the short clause scored by adding punctuation at the end of 7:1b, marks the beginning of Paul's reply with 7:2a. Even the use of verse numbers added later in the production of the text follows this early and persistent rescoring of the continuous script. The short phrase at 2a in the neutral script is scored as to fall outside the quotable phrase concerning "It is not good for a man to touch a woman." And so, the clause separated from the previous phrase is left to be associated with what follows. The clause διὰ δὲ τὰς πορνείας is commonly rendered "because of" illicit or unsanctioned intercourse. And so separated from what preceded by the conventions of reading and punctuation, the clause "Because of illicit sex" is scored in the common sentential order as opening Paul's reply to the preceding quote from Corinth. The force of the phrase "Because of πορνειας" as the introductory frame of Paul's own reply serves to influence the status of sexual relations between a husband and wife. In other words, "Each man should have his own wife and each woman her own husband ... because of illicit sex."

I propose we first consider a reading of Paul's reply as beginning at 7:2b rather than at 7:2a. I argue that beginning with 7:2b and following produces a reading which presents a very straight forward egalitarian discourse concerning sexual relations between husband and wife. Re-scoring of the script by moving the clause at 7:2a out of Paul's reply would read:

> Each man should have his own wife and each woman her own husband. 3 The husband should give to his wife her conjugal rights, and likewise the wife to her husband. 4 For the wife does not have authority over her own body, but the husband does; likewise, the husband does not have authority over his own body but the wife does.

Husband and wife should each have their own heterosexual mate, each has conjugal rights, and each rules over the body of the other. Thus, we have a conflict to consider between the quoted claim that "it is good for a man not to touch a woman," and "Each man should have his own wife and each woman her own husband ..." which are separated by the clause "because of illicit sex."

Well in the classical reading, clearly articulated in the work of Tertullian and Jerome, the short phrase at 7:2a which separates these two very different systems of valuation serves to adjudicate the ambiguity under the persuasion of their discursive venture by rescoring the continuous script. In the Greek the text reads

> 1Co 7:1 περι δε ων εγραψατε καλον ανθρωπω γυναικος μη απτεσθαι
> Concerning (δε) which you wrote Good for a man not to touch a woman
>
> 1Co 7:2a δια δε τας πορνειας
> Because of πορνειας
>
> 7:2b εκαστος την εαυτου γυναικα εχετω
> Each man should have his own wife and each woman her own husband.

Jerome clearly presents the clause at verse 2a as opening and framing Paul's reply. He writes,

> Because of πορνειας each man should have his own wife and each woman her own husband.

One of the things I find troubling is that given the established sentential order by means of the addition of punctuation, the use of the particle δε[7] in 7:2a is made to conform to the already common orthodox reading of the script. "Good for a man not to touch a woman" concludes with a period. And the clause that follows the common quotation (δια δε τας πορνειας) introduces Paul's reply. The particle δε can serve to mark the conversation moving ahead to the next topic or may mark the offering of an explanation to a claim or serve to intensify the content of a claim.

I argue that the clause at 7:2a (δια δε τας πορνειας: because of illicit sexual intercourse) may be read as completing the quotation copied by Paul at verse 1b. If the quotation concerning the matter about which you wrote begins at 1b and concludes with 2a, then the full quotation is a complete, cohesive articulations of a coherent position concerning heterosexuality as illicit.

The full quotation as drawn by Paul as a "sentence" from the missive addressed to him from Corinth, could be rescored to support the following reading:

> Περι δε ων εγραψατε καλον ανθρωπω γυναικος μη απτεσθαι δια δε τας πορνειας.
>
> Concerning what you wrote:
> It is good for a man not to touch a woman because of πορνειας.

Given the Greek syntax, I offer a different reading which emphasizes the reason as a prominent feature of the quotation by a change in word order.

> Concerning what you wrote:
> Because of πορνειας it is good for a man not to touch a woman.

All heterosexual relations are illicit and therefore not good. In the common discourse which influences the scoring of the biblical text, no mention is made

---

7 The particle δε is a primary particle (adversative or continuative); but, and, etc.:—also, and, but, moreover, now [and is often unexpressed in English translations].

of the effect of such illicit behavior as being "no good for a woman." It is apparently the case that male erotic desire per se is not stigmatized, rather a man touching a woman is *illicit*. No mention is made of the marital status of the man and women engaged in sexual contact. Simply put sexual touching is *porno* to use the anglicized phonetic rendering of the root Greek term of πορνειας.

With this rendering of the reading the uses of the particle δε at 7:1a and in the clause at 7:2a serve two different purposes.

> 1Co 7:1–2a   Περι δε ων εγραψατε καλον ανθρωπω γυναικος μη απτεσθαι δια δε τας πορνειας
>
> Concerning (δε) what you wrote it is good for a man not to touch a woman because (δε) of πορνειας.

I contend that on the rendition I propose, the negative particle δε at 7:1a conveys Paul's adversarial posture in introducing the quoted claim from the Corinthians. In the concluding clause of the Corinthian quotation, the particle δε was part of the argument quoted from the Corinthian correspondence to Paul and served in their argument to provide an intense clarification concerning the reason behind the position they posed to Paul. The matter about which some in the Corinthian congregation wrote to Paul assessed that all heterosexual touching is illicit. On this reading, Paul is not advocating FOR the quote "Good for a man not to touch a woman because of illicit sex" which he has drawn from the Corinthian correspondence addressed to him. Rather, he indicates in his use of the negative particle δε not his advocacy of the quote in his introduction at 7:1a, but his adversarial posture.

Paul's counter claim and critique to the quoted claim at 1b through 2a, on this rendition of the script so scored, begins with verse 2b. The placement of the negative particle in the introduction serves to tip off the reader on how to read what follows. I speculate that the congregation on hearing the script read aloud by a well-trained reader, would understand in the reading performance that Paul is quoting what was written as an opportunity for his critical engagement. To perform the introduction such that the quotation is adversarial would be to read the quote with a tone indicative of the status of the quoted matter so as to signal the transition from quote to critique, position proposed to counter position.

But such a reading, involving my decision to place the period after the first clause in verse 2, would on Augustine's criteria, be making a heretical distinction in the script which serves to establish sentences which are not in keeping with orthodoxy or the rule of faith. And of course, Augustine would be

THE SENSE OF QUOTING   69

correct. Such punctuation runs counter to the rule of faith. But Augustine may be incorrect, for the rule of faith is an ambiguous control which is the product of an institutional process which establishes conventional rules in service to institutional ideology.

Recall that it was Augustine who declared that the rule of faith would be supported if not determined by the presence of plainer passages and in consideration of the authority of the church. But in this case, the plainer passage is a quote drawn from another text and author which Paul quotes in his own missive reply to the Corinthian congregation. So, in what sense is the quote from Verse 7:1b "It is good for a man not to touch a woman" a plainer text on Augustine's terms? Is the phrase a plainer text because there is general agreement as to the status, construction of the phrase out of the continuous script, and the meaning of the phrase?

For Augustine, ambiguity in the script should be considered in relation to the plainer passages in providing options for how to best "distinguish" sentential order and how to "perform" the script such that it makes sense in concert with the plainer phrases. The decision as to how to appoint the neutral script to fulfill the desire to design sentential order may be too quickly resolved when the pressure is to influence what phrases might be harvested as pericopes in the production of quotation for discursive purposes rather than the pursuit to converse about how to read the script.

The verses in English translation as rescored from the neutral script produces two alternative appointments of the script which result in two different ways to read how the script articulates.

> Now concerning what you wrote,
>   "It is good for a man not to touch a woman."
> Because of πορνειας each man should have his own wife and each woman her own husband.
>
> Now concerning what you wrote,
>   "It is good for a man not to touch a woman because of πορνειας."
> Each man should have his own wife and each woman her own husband.
>
> Re-scored Standard Rendition of Extended Script 1 Cor 7:1–6
>
> Concerning what you wrote
>   "It is good for a man not to touch a woman."
> (Paul's reply) But because of πορνειας let each man have his own wife and let each woman have her own husband. The husband must fulfill his

obligations to his wife and likewise the wife to her husband. The wife does not have authority over her own body, but her husband does. And likewise, also the husband does not have authority over his own body, but the wife does. Do not defraud one another except perhaps by agreement for a time, in order that you may devote yourselves to prayer, and then you should be together again, lest Satan tempt you because of your lack of self-control.

Rescored Alternative Rendition of Extended Script 1 Cor 7:1–6

Concerning (δε) what you wrote
"It is good for a man not to touch a woman because (δε) of πορνειας."
OR, "Because of πορνειας it is good for a man not to touch a woman."
(Paul's reply) Let each man have his own wife and let each woman have her own husband. The husband must fulfill his obligations to his wife and likewise the wife to her husband. The wife does not have authority over her own body, but her husband does. And likewise, also the husband does not have authority over his own body, but the wife does. Do not defraud one another except perhaps by agreement for a time, in order that you may devote yourselves to prayer, and then you should be together again, lest Satan tempt you because of your lack of self-control.

A few things to note. First, the shift of the period from placement immediately following "women" in the standard rescored English translation of the text to following πορνειας to mark the termination of the quote presents that it is good for a man not to touch a woman because the touch is πορνειας. Thus, Paul's reply begins at 2b with the declaration of marriage as an agreement, if not a contract of mutual consent and mutual domination with an emphasis on a couple's sexual relations. With this shift in which the script is punctuated, πορνειας *as* sexual immorality is attached or associated with the quote which justifies the celibacy of a man as an avoidance of sexual immorality, and not with marriage as a means for the avoidance of some form of sexual immorality.

With the shift of the period and change of sentential order, Satan's temptation addressed later in Paul's reply is no longer associated with πορνειας as it was associated in the standard rendition. Rather, Satan's temptation concerns the temptation to "defraud" the terms of marriage. To avoid this defrauding, if they choose to abstain by mutual consent for a season of pray, they are to come together again, that is, return to their co-dominating sexual relationship as husband and wife lest Satan tempt one or both not to return to their sexual relationship because of a lack of self-control. And it is at this point that the opposition against the quoted claim that it is good for a man not to touch a woman stands forth in greater relief as the target of Paul's critique and provides the reader with a sense of who might be the agent in the marriage who would be tempted.

I find Paul's wording at this point more direct as it would appear that he is writing directly to husbands and wives among his assumed audience as "you"—

> Do not defraud one another except perhaps by agreement for a time, in order that you may devote yourselves to prayer, and then you should be together again, lest Satan tempt you because of your lack of self-control.

So the status of the separation to effect a married couple's sexual relation during a time of prayer serves to defraud one another. Such defrauding of the terms of marriage should only be done for a limited separation by mutual agreement for purposes of prayer. Apparently mutually agreed upon defrauding their marriage agreement for a time so long as they return to the proper if not formal state of co-dominating sexual relations thereby resolves their mutual defrauding. And it is at this point in the extended text that the conception of temptation is introduced. For in their separation from one another by mutual consent for prayer during which both parties defraud their marriage agreement and one another, Satan might tempt one or both (again egalitarian) "because of a lack of self-control."

What has this to do with the claim that "It is good for a man to not touch a woman because of sexual immorality"? Might the identification of their sexual relationship as πορνειας by the male partner result from a temptation born of his lack of self-control as he pursues his own purification by means of his defrauding the terms of marriage with his wife? For it is good for a man not to touch a woman. On Paul's terms on the rescored script such a separation motivated by a man who seeks consecration by means of celibacy would require the husband to defraud his wife. The husband owes his wife his obedience to her sexual domination of his body. For the husband to deny his wife domination over his body, to fail to fulfill his responsibility to his wife, would be to defraud his marriage vows-covenant-contract with his wife.

So, what is the temptation raised in verse 5? Well on the standard classical reading still dominant in Roman Catholic interpretation the temptation is first and foremost sexual immorality which is committed when a man and a woman engage in sexual relations. Therefore, as regards the temptation with respect to a married couple raised in verse 5, for the standard classical scoring of the text in keeping with the defense of the male celibacy interpretation based on the appointing of the terminus of the quote at the end of verse 1, the standard interpretation must reintroduce or return to πορνειας in verse 2a as the temptation by Satan raised later in the text in verse 5. The incorporation of the phrase "because of πορνειας" at verse 2 with the discussion of the mutual sexual domination of husband and wife as the purpose of marriage, must then be glossed over on the standard interpretation. That is, if it is good for a man not to touch a woman, then how is it the case that marriage is accommodated to avoid πορνειας? This was of course the point made by Jerome who declared that if it is good for a man to not touch a woman, then it was bad for a man to touch a woman. And while marriage was tolerated, so as to avoid πορνειας, marriage was nevertheless not a good. That is, the sexual desire and satisfaction of a married couple were on Jerome's account, bad if not evil. Sex in marriage was simply a compromise. For Jerome apparently at best a compromise with evil.

And if a husband or wife wandered from their marriage bed satisfying their sexual desire with another, then such was πορνειας. Thus, on Jerome's terms, if Paul cautioned the married couple not to over extend their mutually agreed upon abstinence to avoid temptation, the temptation born of abstinence for the married couple was for one or the other to commit πορνειας in the breach of their marriage. And that breach violated the reason for the compromise to allow marriage in the first place … on the standard reading and rescoring of the script.

Thus, sexual relations between husband and wife is not the cause of temptation, which is the result of the standard rescoring of the neutral script as defined by the use of the phrase "because of sexual immorality" which is rendered in the standard Christian discourse as Paul's introduction to his own position regarding heterosexual marriage. Thus the text so scored, sexual immorality is deployed to introduce Paul's reply and to so frame what follows such that a reader might by a simple but questionable association with the phrase warning against temptation, conclude that the temptation has to do with sexual immorality whereby a spouse who is not being satisfied in the marriage because his or her spouse in seeking consecration by means of abstinence, may seek sexual satisfaction outside the marriage. The classical standard rescoring of the text and the interpretation it supports is a convoluted discourse which seeks to manage a text which possesses a valued quotable phrase in support of male celibacy for religious, social and political reasons. The rescoring and supported interpretation institutes a discourse in support of the devaluation of human sexuality, marriage and especially women, in order to establish social, political and economic advantages for celibate men through an ideology of Christian consecration as reserved exclusively for those men who are not compromised by women.

The classical scoring of the text produces a reading which fails to play out the articulations and cohesiveness of the extended concrete ancient manuscripts of Paul's letters to the Corinthians. The alternative I propose is that it is the agreed upon abstention for prayer which may lead to a temptation such that separated, the husband (in keeping with the quoted matter as rescored at 7:1b–2a) comes to the conclusion that consecration is being obtained or has been obtained in some significant sense by means of his sexual abstinence with his wife. On this reading of the alternative rescoring of the script the temptation concerns the man who defrauds the marriage partner in seeking or believing that he is attaining his own consecration as an individual man. In the association of abstinence and consecration in the classical reading and scoring of the script, the husband's sexual relations with a wife renders the wife as the contaminate which compromises if not forecloses the possibility of the husband's own individual sense of consecration. Marital sexuality forecloses the possibility of a man's desire for consecration and the advantages and benefits which come with a man not associating with a woman. In other words, for the man seeking his own consecration, sexual relations with his wife would be immoral sexuality (to play on the inclusion of 7:2a as the concluding reason for the claim that "it is good for a man not to touch a woman).

So, on the reading of the alternative rescored text, the Devil's temptation is for the man who while abstaining from marital relations for a season of prayer comes to agree, believe and act in accord with the quotation that "it is good for a man not to touch a woman because of πορνειας." And so, preferring his own consecration the man "defrauds" on his own covenant with his wife. While not explicitly stated it would seem that such a defrauding would also stigmatize the wife as the agent of desecration.

Or, possibly the quoted phrase concerning that it is good for a man not to touch a woman *because of* πορνειας, might play out the figurative sense of the term as idolatry. For a man in pursuit of consecration by abstention, sexual relations with his wife may be valued as his choosing his desire for sexual relations with a woman over sexual abstinence required for a consecrating relationship with God. Thus, the alternative extension of the quote to include "because of πορνειας" provides for a cohesive reading in which the quotation so cultivated and identified, is played out in detail in Paul's negative discursive engagement with the quote. Male abstinence and the avoidance of a marital sexual relations for the sake of one's own advantage as consecrated is presented in Paul's reply not as a temptation of πορνειας, but as a husband *defrauding* his wife.

On the standard reading persuaded by Tertullian and Jerome, the temptation by Satan was aligned with the clause at verse 2a concerning sexual immorality which they took as the introduction of Paul's response. So framed the quotation concerning male consecration was "sentenced" (judgment) as a complete thought which served as the introduction to Paul's theme and his position for what followed with his response to the claim that "it is good for a man not to touch a woman" concluding with Paul's statement "This I say by way of concession, not of command" (7:6). But the status of verse 6 is itself ambiguous as to the direction in the text which Paul is qualifying with regards to "This I say". For if verse 6 is now pivoting from the question regarding the status of sexual relations of a married couple as regards the quoted matter "It is good for a man not to touch a woman because of πορνειας," then the pivot is Paul's introduction to his expression of personal preferences to follow which proceeds through the end of the chapter. Paul's repeated clarification that what begins at verse 6 is qualified as his opinion, his "saying" as opposed to "a saying" which is authoritative, as in speaking for the Lord, or repeating or quoting the Lord. Tertullian and Jerome and those who were influenced by their interpretation, identified and cultivated the pericope drawn from the "matter" quoted from the Corinthians in verse 1b, as the theme and position of Paul's reply to the Corinthians in what followed concerning sexuality and consecration. Thus, the pivotal phrase at verse 6, "This I say by way of concession, not of command" in Tertullian and Jerome's rescoring of the text serves to limit the status of what preceded beginning with the phrase "Because of sexual immorality" concerning marriage and following through to the end of the chapter. In other words, the prized pericope stands as a command, while what follows is Paul's opinion.

On the alternative appointing I propose the quoted verse includes the reason for why it was good for a man not to touch a woman because of πορνειας, whether it be sexually illicit or in a more figuratively sense "because of πορνειας" as idolatry. What follows the πορνειας as illicit on this alternative reading results in a stinging reply in keeping with rabbinic critique of a husband who seeks consecration by abstaining from relations with his wife. Such abstention from relations defrauds the conditions and terms of marriage, as well as the wife's rights and authority. But on my read, Paul goes so far as to characterizes such pious asceticism of a married man as the influence of temptation. The married man who believes that it is good for a man not to touch a woman because it is illicit or idolatry, pursues his own advantage at a most grieves cost to his wife. For a wife is framed as the counter force to her husband's consecration (Odell-Scott 2005, 223–224).

Such an institution would be tantamount to the establishment of a social-political system in which women would be identified as temptations, as desecrations to men seeking consecration. And of course, this did happen and continues to happen. The discourse which deployed the cultivated conventional pericope at 7:1b, was employed to declare that all heterosexual relations between men and women even within the bounds of marriage as at best a compromise provided to avoid even greater illicit promiscuity, and bar any man who was so married from serving in any consecrated ecclesiastical office. The discourse driven by delusions of male megalomania and misogyny has served and influenced Christian theocratic institutionalization persistently and pervasively.

Concluding the Question of Plainer Passages: Augustine and the Persistence of Semiotic Issues

Augustine's concern to address and resolve what he assessed as ambiguity in the script in *On Christian Teaching* was identified as first a sentential problem to be resolved by the use of marks of punctuation and second an issue to be resolved by a reading performance of the script. Umberto Eco's notions of open and closed text suggests to me that Augustine may well have understood the scale on which the scriptures were open (Eco 1981). For it was the degree to which the manuscripts are open that was an underlying concern in Augustine's semiotic efforts to affect the scoring of the script and to influence the reading performance of the text. Augustine's harsh judgment of those who demarcate or distinguish the sentences differently by use of points added to the script, provides opportunity for the production of drawn *sententia* from a source which as Eco might suggest serve as tokens of the venerated source work with all the associated rhetorical value and authority of the text. The formalized rule which guided Augustine's choices was to fashion the script's sentential order and influence the effective reading performance such that the script would be in keeping with orthodox Christianity as established by the decrees of the ecumenical councils. Augustine's judgment was against all readings and scoring of the texts in the production of a sentential order which on his terms aided the enemies of the orthodox rule of faith. Heretical demarcating distinctions were presented as "inadequate" or "inappropriate" or "wrong," and so served Augustine's endeavor to disqualify alternative fabrication of sentential order which or would threaten the authority and exclusive control over how scripture would be read. For Augustine, Orthodox Christianity has proprietary rights as regards the production of the drawing of orthodox *sententia* for Orthodox Christian use, distribution, and reception in teaching, preaching and worship. Had the script been coded in such a way as to show a strong tendency to encourage a particular reading which admitted no further interpretation, producing what some theorist assess to be a high degree of redundancy, there would have been no contest regarding punctuation or reading performance (Eco 1981, 170). Such a text would have been structurally simpler if not "over coded."

I took issue with Augustine's method for resolving phrasing he judged as producing ambiguous readings by identifying and employing phrases assessed as plainer to provide guidance on interpreting the more difficult phrases. But, Augustine's pivot to the plainer phrases as providing evidence on how to illuminate what the more difficult phrases mean belies the point that the status of such phrases "as plainer" are themselves already the products of re-fabrication. The phrases are plainer and produce clarity only in so far as the script has already been rescored. For what is "plainer" and therefore quotable for providing guidance is the yield of a text which has been manufactured such that the passages now appear as forthright and clear statements. Augustine's appeal to the "plainer" passages is a magician's trick, the rhetorical equivalent of an act of misdirection. The manipulation is already underway and passes unseen.

The issue, to put it plainly is that under the persuasion of the dominant ideology of western Christian orthodoxy, the habits of reading the scriptures are already established and served to master and discipline the punctuation and articulations of the script such that the *textus* of the manuscripts before rescoring and their potential for alternative reading renditions are often of little influence in the decisions concerning punctuation and performance of the script. The motivations for such mastery and discipline of the scripture are done to insure a favorable selection in the harvesting, production and deployment of quotations in service to one's own ecclesial agenda. Influencing the introduction of punctuation into the script often serves to articulate a theological and convictional agenda without regard for, let alone respect for the *textus* of the work which is being parsed, demarcated, articulated and harvested for suitable quotations. So demarcated and articulated, the classical reading is recorded back into the script, and the script is employed for the schooling of the faith such that the determined reading of the text becomes a naturalized reading in the church. I argue that this mastery is little more than the remastery of a set of scripts, a recoding or encoding of a performance which seeks to provide the signs for reading and the passing on of a habit for how to perform the script, punctuating and articulating a sentential order for a desired effect so as to control what may be said, heard, thought, felt, and understood with respect to the script.

The bringing of those complicated renegade verses into disciplined compliance with the rescoring and established remastery of the script is a means for tying up loose ends. What does one do with the remnants of the script after the prized pericopes have been cut out? Are these remnants to be ignored or swept up off the cutting floor as production waste? Some forms of Christian teaching and preaching, like conducting a magic act, entails mastering how to direct the attention of the audience such that they unknowingly look and take notice of that which the performer of magic wants them to see, all the while hiding the manipulation of selection so that what appears to be surprisingly if not magically connected, illuminating, and revealing, is simply just another trick. For in reading performance, such magic, illumination and revelatory experience are effects of the semiotic and rhetorical manipulation of a text. And so what remains of the *textus* is rendered invisible to the eye as one moves on, or tracks where the teacher or the preacher wants one to look.

Given the authority ascribed to or acknowledged of the scriptures, the contest over whose sense of the script will dominate is an open and ongoing debate, if not an open conflict. Whose favorite quotes are evident in the phrasing and protected by the sentential ordering and translation of the script are matters of debate, contest, and competition. For Augustine, the competition concerned how he and the Christianity he championed would succeed if others controlled how the script was marked and quoted. The decisions concerned not so much the status of the texture of the work, as it concerned for Augustine, his contemporary compatriots and adversaries, and the economy of advantages for their cause. For the contest was about rhetorical persuasion between alternative theological Christian approaches, and the institutions and communities which were aligned with each approach.

A problem is that a phrase as quoted and paraded as a plainer text which serves to support the establishment of an ecclesiastical theocracy dominated by a celibate all-male hierarchy remains ambiguous as to the sense of a drawn quote even in the immediate verses which are related. For what follows from such an analysis exhibits multiple ambiguities each of which are suggestive of a very different sense of the cohesiveness, coherence and articulation of the text, at least the text in its local presentation if not the greater *textus* of the epistle.

Under the persuasion of classical rhetoric, the sense of a quotation was to serve some positive purpose, to support in the moral and personal growth and development of the privileged educated young men in Greek and Roman society and so internalize the codes of the elite. Quotations from works valued among society's privileged serve to establish one's own place and to enhance one's arguments in keeping with what is assumed to be proper manners, proper values, proper education and so to punctuate one's standing and influence those who read one's works or listened to one's oration.

The presumptions as regards one's own privilege was that other works from which one would borrow or draw forth quotations would be harvested for one's own store. The sense of a quote was to support one's own discourse. For given the privilege of the elite, the entitled, other works of importance and value were to be drawn for one's own good, one's own cause, and to make one's own case.

Those trained in the schools of rhetoric, formally trained who often in turn taught rhetoric, assumed their privileged vantage point, and a sense of entitlement, even as they came to practice and to strive for rank among the faithful in Christianity. Christians trained in the arts of rhetoric thus sought to draw upon borrowed material, such that their own cause, their own position, their own privilege and entitlement would be enhanced and supported by the use of quotations even drawing upon what was recorded as having been said by Jesus, or what was written by the Apostle Paul.

Thus under the pervasive and persistent social, economic, and cultural hierarchies in which they thrived and competed and flourished, the patriarchs of the church trained in the arts of rhetoric adapted their pursuits, and oft employed their training in these pursuits as their own ends—clothed in what they took to be a new order of things, a spiritualization in which they sought yet once again the privilege of their own cause, striving for prestige and rank in the new hierarchies of Christianity and the church. And so Christian rhetorical endeavors under the old influences of classical rhetoric and its effective culture and social hierarchy became the tool for those who held themselves in such high regard that their reading and comprehension of the faith was assumed to be privileged. And so they prosecuted their cause to influence and further their social and political commitments by means of the old methods, drawing quotes out of scripts, even sacred writ as suited their endeavors.

Such desire among so many who declared their faith as if their own desire were itself slayed. Such hubris. Yet hubris morphed under the persuasion of a desire for individual male consecration by means of ascetic ascent. And so these masters of Christian rhetoric crafted the neutral script so as to sanction *their* "delusional fantasies of sanctity" and stigmatized *Eros* (Odell-Scott 2005, 222). And yet, these men, Christian men, sought to satisfy their own grandest desire and designed an ascetic social-political system for individual male sanctification by means of egotistical striving presented as not egotistic and as not a striving. And so their fashioned quotes presented their desires, their striving for sacred privilege, their designs on theocratic entitlements, in support of men who declared their forsaking of desire.

The sense of a much-quoted phrase in a meta-narrative comes to be understood within the discourse to the exclusion of how the phrase may appear or function within a source text from which it was drawn and quoted so long as the institutional rhetorical discourse holds persuasion. For reading under the persuasion of a naturalized discourse if not in keeping with a culture's meta-narrative, is to read a text without regard for how the source text is a cohesive tissue which so moves the reader of the materialized language on the page. Thus how the source is textured beyond the sense provided by the meta-narrative fades from the view of the reader. For it is not so much that the text falls apart into discreet sentences which fail to exhibit cohesiveness and coherence in their relation to one another. It is because the text's texture must be hidden such that articulations which discourage or possibly disrupt the naturalized narrative simply pass unseen. It is as if the text was only conveyed by means of quotations supplied to and incorporated in the meta-discursive-narrative. Such conditioned reading renders the effective source text as if it were known in total by means of the harvested quotations, and thus emptied of further content. Thus explained away or simply replaced by the explanatory power of the discourse for the determination of the status, value and content of the quotations, the text is used up as if there were nothing more to read, to review, to consider or with which to play. For the textures and the articulations of the *textus*, now erased or hidden by the discursive meta-narrative masters its quotations and the sources of its quotations. For all that is needed of the biblical texts are the pericopes which once harvested in support of the discursive meta-narratives, renders what remains of the text as little more than the mutilated ruminants which are swept up off the preverbal cutting floor and discarded as rubbish.

Concluding Considerations
Pragmatics

With the passing of the associates of an exchange of letters, with only the composite epistles composed by one party that includes quotations from the other parties to attest to the structures and content of their exchange, the extra-textual milieu in which the material contemporary letters circulated and which they were composed—is lost. Our only record of these protracted personal engagements within the complex social and historical circumstances are the letters. Much if not most of the plays of denotation and connotation in the exchange, as well as the structures and textures of the articulations within the material exchange of letters and the oral performance of reporting who and what was said, including the use of catch phrases and quotations associated with if not attributed to persons and social groupings, the contests between various groups over differing convictions (not to mention the differences concerning broader social, political, economic and culture differences which influenced alliances and contests) and all the rich subtitles which influence the sense of such composition and communication have faded in time if not faded out. All who composed, transcribed, conveyed, read or heard the letters which was addressed to them, all who spoke and reported on what was said are dead. And they have been dead for almost two millennia. The only traces of their exchange, and maybe of all of their lives (with the exception of Paul) are the letters of Paul. So, the rich *textus* of these epistolary scripts are lost on other readers, all other readers. We may wonder at what all is lost on us as we read and imagine the exchanges conveyed in these purloined letters between long dead associates.

The material transcription that survives the context and production persists as a text reduced, for all that remains are the scripts. The material *textus* was composed using specific technologies and techniques, under the influence of associated operational codes and ciphers in the expressing, composing and performance of an exchange which are themselves to such a considerable degree now faded and thin.

With the attrition of the parties involved and the loss of both the broader social and cultural context, as well as the micro-social and micro-cultural contexts which influence various local or personal codes and signs, and as well with changes in technologies and techniques, other legacies of semiosis provide chains of association which over time produce codes and add signs for making sense of the script. Thus semiotic chains of association so produced in the subsequent re-encoding and rescoring by means of interpretative interplay of readers proceed under the persuasion of later social and cultural influences contemporary with readers and their interpretative ventures.

The reliance on the material work of course increases as the context of composition and the parties involved pass away. Further loss of the context of composition concerns changing social and cultural milieu such that use of technologies and techniques for expressing and representing, and different codes and signs in operation to capture the sense of the work are assumed whether correctly or incorrectly for decoding the script in subsequent reading and performance. And these changing technologies and techniques, codes and conventions which effect readings, scoring, quoting and discursive ventures, also inevitable fade as well. Often such discursive endeavors also pass as attrition takes its toll. Features of these legacies of semiosis often morph under the persuasion of other technologies and techniques, codes and signs, which also in their time change and fade. The complex and often contentious and contesting plays of the plurality of chains of semiosis concerning the script rise and recede effecting the reading and performance of the script in the production of rescored and remastered texts. The sense of a work, or the sense of its *textus* are always under reconsideration and reconstruction as the script is received in the life of semiotic play through history and cultures, and as the technological changes in production as well as changes in the techniques of scoring and performance transfer a rendition of the text and pass on a sense made of it.

A philosophical question, which is more than a simple problem, concerns whether in any clear or strong sense each work titled as an epistle and attributed to Paul is singular or, by means of the legacy of semiotic chains of signification, each presents a different rendition so scored and mastered: is there little more than a family resemblance among the lot?

Post-Script

On a Peircean model of semiotics any sign is ideally available for an infinite process of semiosis. The production of unbridled chains of signs playing off the wild potentials of semiosis has the potential of signifying anything and everything imaginable for every imaginable purpose. And yet, while such wild semiosis offers the possibility of an infinite process of signification, the issue raised in Peircean thought is: "For what purpose?"

The coherence which comes with semiosis ala Peirce is occasioned if not driven by the pragmatics of the semiotic activity. Wild semiosis while a possibility cannot be incorporated into a coherent semiotic system which in Peircean thought is a precondition for the possibility of critical or scientific inquiry. But coherent semiotic systems need not be attached or refer or correspond to a physical, historic or existential reality. While coherence is a precondition on Peircean semiotics for the possibility of critical or scientific inquiry, coherence may obtain and persist much like the creative works of arts and literature which play upon operational codes and ciphers in their composition and reception that are valued for their expressive and imaginative effect. And as regards effect, such effects of such coherent semiotic systems may serve a purpose, which become the field of evidence for critical or scientific inquiry.

Critical discourse analysis proceeds by addressing this query concerning "purpose" as a portal for considering how semiosis fuels particular discourses in the struggle to not simply have one's say, or express one's imaginative sign play, but to influence and effect the discursive narrative of social and political institutions.

On the Peircean model the triadic interactions among the (1) representamen, (2) an object and (3) an interpretant, the representamen of the signage and its object represents nothing without an interpretant. Given that the interpretant serves to focus on selected features which instigate a signifying relation of representamen and object, it is the interpretant that in effect connects the representamen to the object.[8] Cohesiveness and coherence are purposeful productions (Odell-Scott and Aiecher 2013).

---

8   This semiotic function concerns how the energy to actualize semiosis is produced. And while it would not be wrong to understand this energy as somehow "subjective" (as Whitehead explicitly does), it would be something of a philosophical category mistake to attribute such "subjectivity" *only* to human persons, groups or species (or animals universally). The sense of

That an interpreter proceeds to address the array of interpretations which any biblical text might suggest is one thing, but unless the interpreter selects which feature or topic or theme in the text is to be addressed, semiosis does not progress. The object of course must exhibit features which can be drawn upon by the interpreter in the process of signification (differentiated by Peirce as three different categories of operation as "iconic," "indexical" and "symbolization") as drawn by the interpreter to provide content for the sign-from or for the object. For all processes of signification on a Peircean model entail the triadic pattern of interactions among an "interpretant," an "object" and "representamen" in which the "interpretant" makes or occasions the connections between object and sign. Signs signify a signified for a signifier.

The restraints upon the possibility of a wild semiosis depend upon a connection established between sign-chains and the processes of critical ends directed inquiry. The processes of critical ends directed inquiry is also on Peircean grounds, a triadic patter of interactions among an "interpretant" that restricts the possible connections of object and sign such that the chains of signs produced might tend towards a definite idealized end such that the possibility of complete knowledge of a semiotic object might be pursued.

Given the richness of features evident or generated by analysis the return by the signifier to a semiotic "object" for further critical inquiry is the idealized pursuit of complete knowledge of the "semiotic object." In this sense the classic definition of a sign as signifying something else or more, trends towards signifying more of the object of inquiry. But the completion of such inquiry may never attain satisfaction if one takes seriously the highly refined process semiotic thought of Alfred North Whitehead (Whitehead 1922 and 1978).

Eco contends that between the positions regarding the claim (1) that any text can be interpreted only in one way according to the intention of its author and (2) that a text supports every interpretation without regard for the intention of its author, lies a "recorded thesaurus of encyclopedic competence, a social storage of world knowledge, and on these grounds, and only on these grounds, any interpretation can be both implemented and legitimated ..." (Eco 1984, 3). That is, the implementation and legitimation of any interpretation has to do with the selection and use of a feature which is drawn from the text as an object of inquiry. Thus, between what we take to be the intention of the text's author and how a text has been interpreted to support every interpretation without regard for the intention of its author lies the "record" of all that a text might mean. Only in consulting this record of all possible meanings and

---

an interpretant is exhibited for instance by operational codes and ciphers (which may concern machine semiotic activity) or closer to this thesis, interpretant as institutional ideology.

interpretations, a virtual "thesaurus" of possible interpretations, one might proceed to consider what the text may "bare". But Eco's "archive" does not vouch safe any semiosis whether disciplined or wild. The semiotic grounds of implementation and legitimacy of any interpretation lies in the engagement of Eco's "archive" characterized as a "recorded thesaurus of encyclopedic competence." I take it that less we proceed by an examination of the archive of the text's reception, interpretation, implementation and legitimation through the institutions of history and culture by which the possibilities of a text's meanings have been actualized and tested, how else are we to critically engage the close and careful analysis of a work?

Signs signify a signified for a signifier. And the search for signification (and in some instances reference) has the potential of achieving satisfaction only as regards an idealized end to a coherent sign chain. The use of a text which has been actualized through discursive venture in the influence of social and political institutions, establishes for critical discourse analysis the competency of the text for critical evaluation. That is to say, a text which has influenced the discursive engagements of social and political institutions, and especially when woven into institutional ideology, is a text with standing for analysis and evaluation.

I assessed that a specific quote drawn and harvested from 1 Corinthians concerning the fashioned phrase about it not being good for a man to touch a woman, that came to signify the position of the apostle Paul as identified by Tertullian and Jerome in their discursive ventures for the advantage of an all celibate male clergy to enjoy and exercise ecclesiastical theocratic power and authority, then such a quote-sign would serve as a Peircean "symbol" whose success depended upon the utilization of conventions, habits or laws to connect the quote-sign and its object by these interpreters.[9] And further, this

---

9 The object of the quote-sign in our example was itself an artifact. And the degree to which the quote-sign represents some qualitative feature of its object, the artifact known as the "First Letter to the Corinthians", might suggest that such a quote-sign is an "icon" of its object. However, the feature or features of the quote-as-sign which would qualify as resemblance could if not would be little more than the quote resembles the phrase as found in the text as the object of the "icon." As such, the quote as iconic sign repeats the phrase as a semiotic object. Like the photograph which is an "icon" in that the photograph resembles the person as the object of the photograph, the question is whether the quoting of a phrase is iconic of the object quoted? Does that mean that the quote is iconic of only the specific phrase-artifact or quote as iconic of the text artifact which includes the phrase? Certainly, to some degree the presentation of a quote-as-quoting the bible is "iconic" in the sense that all that is being declared is that the sense of a quote in some sense is a resemblance of the basic physical features of the object (the phrase in the text) for the interpretant.

quote-sign was and is employed and influenced the discursive engagements of social and political institutions. In fact, the selection and interpretations of the text in question (1 Cor 7:1) were fashioned into a coherent institutional body of signs which contributed to a recorded thesaurus of encyclopedic competence, a social storage of knowledge, and so came to dominate the recorded thesaurus of the western churches that the produced phrasing and quote became the record against which implementation and legitimization would be judged. For to this day power and authority in the largest religious institution of Christian is dominated by a socio-political ideology in which the quoted verse is symbolic of the Apostle Paul, his Epistles and Holy Writ. The institution of an all celibacy male theocratic leadership is legitimized by the production of a quoted sentence fashioned and then featured as Paul's position as to the status of heterosexual relations in the letter of Paul to the Corinthians.

The *textus* semiotic issues concern the complexities that arise given that the quotation was constructed for a purpose in Paul's epistle reply to the Corinthians who composed the phrase delivered to and quoted by Paul. We sense where the quote begins at 7:1b, but are confounded as to where it concludes. The sense we make of the quote is the result of our operational codes as we seek to decipher the sense of a complex, cohesive articulating *textus*. As regards the critical discourse analysis of these beginnings of the quote traced in the epistle to the Corinthians, we know precious little about the pretext of the quote among the Corinthian congregants, except what we gather on our own from reading Paul's letters. Distant and divorced from the pragmatic events related to the historic occasion of the letters, we are left with texts, copies of copies, which have been thoroughly remanufactured. What we make of "concerning the matter about what you wrote" and what all subsequent readers have made of such matters, is driven less by the pragmatic context

---

Or, if the quote-as-sign utilizes only some existential or physical connection between itself and its object, is the quote-sign then an "index". Book "indexes" are composed by copying a word or phrase from the physical body of the text which is then printed in the Index along with a page number as to where the printed word is connection to the occurrence of the term on a specific page. Is it the case that a quotation of a phrase harvested as a pericope and copied with citation or attribution in a subsequent discourse, is the utilization of a quote-as-index? Is it the case that all that is meant by the interpretant is that the quote-as-sign indexes the object where the phrase quoted is to be found? Or is this too bookish given the common examples of "a cloud of smoke" indexes that something is burning? As an index, the quote indexes the phrase in the text, but does not convey anything as to the content of the phrase in context of the text. To index is to represent that the phrase copied in the discourse indexes the phrase as located or occurring in the text site without much to do regarding the context of the phrase in the source object as indexed.

of the Corinthian-Paul exchange, less by the syntax and semantics evident in the Greek script, than by the context, conventions, codes and expectations of the readers and interpreters.

That a quote seemed to be credible, that is, given the quoted phrase ascribed to Paul as his position on the matter, in tandem with the general instituted reading and quoting of the epistle which emphasizes that women are to be silent in the churches and subordinate to men, it would make no end of sense that Paul would declare that is good for a man not to touch a woman. And that was and remains the conventional reading of the text. And yet the production of such sense making of the quoted phrasing concerning the silence and subordination of women in church, and the manufactured sense of the quoted phrasing that it is good for a man not to touch a woman, are all heavily influenced by operational codes and social conventions which inform how we read and what we choose to emphasize.

When all is said and done, we begin where maybe we should all begin. We begin by reading. The quotes we draw and weaponized in the discursive battles within and between Christian institutions are the products of texts which have been scored and rescored, written and rewritten, remastered, manufactured and translated. And our quotes are drawn and deployed with certainty and authority to champion our sectarian aspirations.

What I sought to do was disrupt our reading of the letters of Paul as if they are an arsenal of quotations. Too familiar with the quotes as weapons, I would have us consider reading the letters of Paul as foreign and different from what we are accustomed to reading, expecting and finding. And so read and consider the scripts as so foreign that we are perplexed as to what sense to make of our reading. That our discomfort and perplexity might make reading so difficult that in our attention to the *textus* we might forget about quoting scripture. Our desires and dreams of authority, advantage and power might fade before us as we are perplexed, humbled, and possibly convicted by our own faults and failings. We might, at least for a time, take responsibility for our struggles to make sense of the texts as we attempt to read the letters.

Works Cited

Augustine. 1995. *De Doctrina Christiana (On Christian Teaching)* (ed. and trans. R. P. H. Green; Oxford: Clarendon Press).

Barthes, Roland. 1986. *The Rustle of Language* (New York: Hill and Wang).

Barthes, Roland. 1979. "From Work to Text," in J. V. Harari (ed.), *Textual Strategies: Perspectives in Post-Structural Criticism* (Ithaca: Cornell University Press).

De Beaugrande, Robert. 1980. *Text, Discourse, and Process: Towards a Multidisciplinary Science of Texts* (Advances in Discourse Processes 4; Norwood, NJ: Ablex).

De Beaugrande, Robert, and Wolfgang Ulrich Dressler. 1981. *Introduction to Text Linguistics* (New York: Longman).

Blass, Friedrich, and Albert Debrunner. 1961. *A Greek Grammar of the New Testament and Other Early Christian Literature; a Translation and Revision of the ninth-tenth German Edition Incorporating Supplementary Notes of A. Debrunner by Robert W. Funk.* (Chicago and London: The University of Chicago Press).

Brown, T. Julian. 1999. "Punctuation," in *Encyclopaedia Britannica.* (Revised and updated, 2002 and 2007. Accessed www.britannica.com/topic/punctuation, January 14, 2017).

Brown, T. Julian. 1993. *A Paleographer's View: The Selected Writings of Julian Brown* (eds. Janet Bately, Michelle P. Brown and Jane Roberts; London: Harvey Miller Publishers).

Chandler, Daniel. 2002. *Semiotics: The Basics* (New York: Routledge).

Clark, Elizabeth. 1999. *Reading Renunciation: Asceticism and Scripture in Early Christianity* (Princeton, NJ: Princeton University Press).

Denniston, J. D. 1934. *The Greek Particles* (Oxford: The Clarendon Press).

Eco, Umberto. 1979. *The Role of the Reader: Explorations in the Semiotics of Texts* (Bloomington: Indiana University Press).

Eco, Umberto. 1984. *Semiotics and the Philosophy of Language* (Bloomington: Indiana University Press).

Eco, Umberto. 1989. *The Open Work* (Cambridge, MA: Harvard University Press).

Eco, Umberto, with Richard Rorty. Jonathan Culler, and Christine Brooke-Rose. 1992. *Interpretation and Overinterpretation* (Cambridge: Cambridge University Press).

Fairclough, Norman. 2001. *Language and Power* (London and New York: Longman).

Fairclough, Norman. 1995. *Critical Discourse Analysis: The Critical Study of Language* (London and New York: Longman).

Gorlee, Dinda. 1994. *Semiotics and the Problem of Translation: with Special Reference to the Semiotics of Charles S. Peirce* (Amsterdam and Atlanta, GA: Rodopi).

Hall, Stuart. 1980. *Culture, Media, Language: Working Papers in Cultural Studies, 1972–1979* (London: Hutchinson).

Hurd, John C. 1965. *The Origins of 1 Corinthians* (New York: Seabury Press).

Jakobson, Roman. 1990. *On Language* (Cambridge, MA: Harvard University Press).

Jerome. 1893. *Against Jovinianus, Book I* (trans. W. H. Fremantle et al., in NPNF 6, ser. II; Buffalo, NY: Christian Literature Publishing Co. Revised and edited for *New Advent* by Kevin Knight. http://www.newadvent.org/fathers/30091.htm. Accessed January 14, 2017).

Lee, Harper. 1960. *To Kill a Mockingbird* (New York: HarperCollins).

Odell-Scott, David. 1991. *A Post-Patriarchal Christology* (The American Academy of Religion Series 78; Atlanta: Scholars Press).

Odell-Scott, David. 2003. *Paul's Critique of Theocracy: A/Theocracy in Corinthians and Galatians* (London/New York: T & T Clark International).

Odell-Scott, David. 1987. "In Defense of an Egalitarian Interpretation of First Corinthians 14:34–36: A Reply to Murphy-O'Connor's Critique," BTB 17.3: 100–103.

Odell-Scott, David. 1983. "Let the Women Speak In Church: An Egalitarian Interpretation of First Corinthians 14:33b–36," BTB 13.3: 90–93.

Odell-Scott, David. 2005. "Patriarchy and Heterosexual Eroticism: The Question in Romans and Corinthians," in C. Green and Daniel Patte (eds.), *Gender, Tradition and Romans: Shared Ground, Uncertain Borders* (Romans Through History and Cultures Series; New York: T&T Clark).

Odell-Scott, David and George Aiecher. 2013. "Semiotics," in Steven L. McKenzie (ed.), *The Oxford Encyclopedia of Biblical Interpretation* (Oxford/New York: Oxford University Press).

Parkes, M. B. 2008. *Their Hands Before Our Eyes: A Close Look at Scribes* (Aldershot: Ashgate).

Parkes, M. B. 1992. *Pause and Effect: An Introduction to the History of Punctuation in the West* (Aldershot: Scolar Press).

Parkes, M. B. 1991. *Scribes, Scripts and Readers: Studies in the Communication, Presentation and Dissemination of Medieval Texts* (London/Rio Grande: Hambledon).

Perrin, Porter G., George H. Smith and Jim W. Corder. 1968. *Handbook of Current English,* 3rd *Edition* (Glenview: Scott, Foresman and Co.).

Porter, Stanley E. 1995. "Discourse Analysis and New Testament Studies: An Introductory Survey," in Stanley E. Porter and D. A. Carson (eds.) *Discourse Analysis and Other Topics in Biblical Greek.* (JSNTS 113; Sheffield: Sheffield Academic Press Ltd.).

Quintilian. 2006. *Institutio Oratoria, Book 2* (eds. Tobias Reinhardt and Michael Winterbottom; Oxford/New York: Oxford University Press).

Ricoeur, Paul. 2004. *On Translation* (New York: Routledge).

Ricoeur, Paul. 1976. *Interpretation Theory: Discourse and the Surplus of Meaning* (Fort Worth: Texas Christian University Press).

Sloane, Thomas O. (ed.), 2001. *Encyclopedia of Rhetoric* (Oxford/New York: Oxford University Press).

Tertullian. 1956. *Monogamy* (trans. and ann. William P. Le Saint, in *Tertullian, Treatises on Marriage and Remarriage, To His Wife, An Exhortation to Chastity, Monogamy*; Westminster, MD: Newman Press).

Van Den Hoek, Annewies. 1996. "Techniques of Quotation in Clement of Alexandria. A View of Ancient Literary Working Methods," *Vigiliae Christianae* 50.3: 223–243.

Whitehead, Alfred North. 1978. *Process and Reality: An Essay in Cosmology* (corrected edition by David Ray Griffin and Donald W. Sherburne; New York: Free Press.).

Whitehead, Alfred North. 2004. *The Principle of Relativity with Applications to Physical Science* (Mineola: Dover Publications [original, 1922]).

Wittgenstein, Ludwig. 2001. *Philosophical Investigations* (third edition, revised translation by G. E. M. Anscombe; Malden: Blackwell [German original, 1953]).

Wittgenstein, Ludwig. 1961. *Tractatus Logico-Philosophicus* (transl. D. F. Pars & B. F. McGuinnes; London/Henley: Routledge & Kegan Paul [German original, 1921]).